First Things First

Managing your time for maximum performance

■

PATRICK FORSYTH

the Institute of Management
FOUNDATION
PITMAN PUBLISHING

The Institute of Management (IM) is at the forefront of management development and best management practice. The Institute embraces all levels of management from students to chief executives. It provides a unique portfolio of services for all managers, enabling them to develop skills and achieve management excellence. If you would like to hear more about the benefits of membership, please write to Department P, Institute of Management, Cottingham Road, Corby NN17 1TT. This series is commissioned by the Institute of Management Foundation.

For Robin,
A timely associate and a good friend

Pitman Publishing
128 Long Acre, London WC2E 9AN

A Division of Longman Group Limited

First published in Great Britain 1994

© Patrick Forsyth 1994

A CIP catalogue record for this book can be obtained
from the British Library

ISBN 0 273 61428 2 (Cased)
1 3 5 7 9 10 8 6 4 2
ISBN 0 273 60733 2 (Paperback)
1 3 5 7 9 10 8 6 4 2

All rights reserved; no part of this publication may be reproduced, stored in a retrieval system, or transmitted in any form or by any means, electronic mechanical, photocopying, recording, or otherwise without either the prior written permission of the Publishers or a licence permitting restricted copying in the United Kingdom issued by the Copyright Licensing Agency Ltd., 90 Tottenham Court Road, London W1P 9HE. This book may not be lent, resold, hired out or otherwise disposed of by way of trade in any form of binding or cover other than that in which it is published, without the prior consent of the Publishers.

Photoset in Century Schoolbook by
Northern Phototypesetting Co. Ltd., Bolton
Printed and bound in Great Britain
by Bell and Bain Ltd, Glasgow

*The Publishers' policy is to use paper manufactured
from sustainable forests.*

Contents

∎

Foreword v
Preface vii
Acknowledgements ix

1 TIME: A KEY RESOURCE 1
The opportunities and the difficulties

2 ASSESSING YOUR SITUATION 9
First steps towards effective time management

3 GETTING AND STAYING ORGANISED 37
Creating the right time environment

4 CONTROLLING THE TIME WASTERS 60
The inherent difficulties and how to deal with them

5 FIRST THINGS FIRST 75
Setting and sticking to priorities

6 CONTROLLING THE PAPERWORK 87
Making paperwork productive

7 PEOPLE AND MANAGEMENT 105
Working with and controlling others
1 People issues
2 Managing others
3 Meetings (and how to survive them)

8 ON THE MOVE 145
Time management away from the office

Afterword 156
Appendix: Time management forms 163
Postscript 179
Index 181

'The day is of infinite length for him who knows how to appreciate and use it'
GOETHE

Foreword

■

Time can never be used again. What might have been done with it may require time in the future. Fortunately there is a great deal of it, which is why we so often squander it, yet perversely so often we find we have too little of it.

Time is opportunity. Use it wisely and satisfaction is the reward. Use it poorly and frustration can be the outcome. To think that we can totally control our time is a delusion. Too many books have been written which suggest that by following a particular system or set of rules or by establishing a set of personal targets, all our goals and ambitions will be achieved. Life is not like that. From the moment we wake each day our time is beset by conflicting demands. But by developing a sense of how to use time well and what wastes time we can have a large degree of control over that precious commodity. By exercising discipline and by planning we can create space for what is really important in our professional and our private lives.

This book does not set down hard and fast rules nor does it promote a particular time management system. Rather it provides an awareness of the uses and abuses of time and suggests ways in which the reader will find it possible to exercise greater control over their time.

Years ago in Filofax we used an advertising slogan 'Every system is unique because you create it'. We had discovered that what our customers wanted was not a sophisticated system, which told them precisely how to organise their time, but a range of papers including blank ones, around which they could create the time and information system best suited to their needs and their way of working. They could add to it, change it, or stop using parts of it without feeling guilty. So it is with *First things First*. In this book there are hundreds of suggestions on how to improve the use of your time. Some of them you will find very relevant to your particular situation. Others may have little application right now. Choose what works for you and discard that which does not.

FOREWORD

Time, like air, is free; how we use it determines the value we add to it at work or at leisure.

David Collischon
Chairman
Filofax Group plc

Preface

■

'Tomorrow is always the busiest day of the week'
JONATHON LAZEAR

The rationale for a book on time management in this series, which has addressing the core management issues and skills high in its brief, is straightforward: time management is, by any definition, a core skill. For any manager, whatever they do, for every executive, the pressure to achieve is high. The markets for most organisations in the nineties are competitive, change is the order of the day and pressures of all sorts seem unlikely to lessen. Success may be described as coming only through a multitude of factors, not least innovation, creativity and good old-fashioned hard work. It is people ultimately who make organisations succeed and if those people are efficient, effective and productive this makes the chances of that success coming about just a little more likely.

Time management is about working efficiently and effectively to ensure both good productivity and that desired results are achieved. Further, it is about working in a way that allows any other necessary elements to thrive; for example, the person who is struggling, submerged by conflicting priorities and sitting at a desk groaning under the weight of innumerable stacks of paper, is unlikely to find it easy just to get things done, much less to be creative.

Of course, much has been written about time management in the past (a good deal of it insisting that you can only make progress by adopting some branded system and its attendant forms, something that is not the case here) and so it is not claimed that all the ideas here will be new to you. But there are several problems with time management. It is, as most who have addressed it in their own work would confirm, difficult. Old habits die hard. Worse, some of its ideas and principles will not work for you. This may be true, or it may actually be that they will not work without some application, adaption or experiment, which is a different matter altogether. Further, it is a topic without any one permanent solution, there is no one 'right' way to manage your time which will work for everyone and which only needs adopting. Although some principles are basic and will help many, there is no

PREFACE

magic formula and everyone must work out their own way of becoming truly effective in terms of their time.

So, this book sets out both to introduce the topic to those who may not have previously investigated it formally, and to help those wishing to revisit it, and aiming to continue to fine-tune their approaches. It aims to present practical ideas, some of which can be implemented immediately, and to present an overall approach which recognises that time management has to be made to work continuously in a way that reflects the real world and all its trials and tribulations. Ultimately, everyone has to work out their own way of approaching it – one that produces efficiency, yet retains sight of the practicalities of the way any particular job works and preserves sanity into the bargain. If an active review of time management provides even a handful of ideas, it will save you valuable time and produce improved efficiency and a greater likelihood of your objectives, whatever they are, being met. If reading this book prompts you to undertake such a review and subsequently to adopt new habits and work practices, then it will be of practical benefit. If it prompts more radical change, then it is not exaggerating to say it could alter your life. If it prompts any such change, the writing of this book will be worthwhile.

Patrick Forsyth
Touchstone Training & Consultancy
17 Clocktower Mews
London N1 7BB

Acknowledgements

■

Managers and executives work in many different functions within the organisation. Yet all need to address certain common areas; indeed all may need to exercise certain of the key skills. Such core skills can range from the perhaps seeming simplicity of drafting a letter or report, to what, for many, is the daunting complexity of managing finance. A major reason for the existence of this series of books is to provide practical guidance in many matters common to achieving management success. Time management is certainly both a common and a key skill for almost anyone in any kind of organisation.

My own experience is primarily in sales and marketing. Here, as in any other function of business, the pressure to be effective – productive in terms of time management – is just as great as in any other area. So, like many people before me no doubt, as soon as I was established in my career and taking some sort of responsibility, I noticed the pressure on time and began to search around for ways of actively fitting more into less time. I soon found it was more difficult than I thought, but I was lucky in that amongst those I worked with early in my career were some who had the matter well sorted themselves and from whom I learnt a great deal.

Though no one is perfect in this area, and I continue to struggle with bad habits and try to remember to practise what I preach, I like to think that overall the pattern of my working is essentially efficient. I continue to see time management as important, to myself and to others. Indeed these days it is one of the topics on which I conduct courses so I like to think I know something about it, though I continue to welcome any new idea that will help me further. Any effectiveness I do have in this area is less a matter of invention, more it has been accumulated because I have gleaned ideas over the years and built up a way of approaching the planning and organising of my work that suits me. So thanks are due to all those I have met and worked with along the way who have wittingly or unwittingly contributed to my experience and helped me learn more about managing time. In doing so, some have contributed good ideas – others (who shall remain nameless) have exhibited dramatic warning by their behaviour!

ACKNOWLEDGEMENTS

Specifically I would like to thank the following: I am particularly grateful to David Collischon, Chairman of Filofax Group plc, who kindly wrote the Foreword, and to the Filofax Group plc for their assistance and specific permission to reproduce a number of forms from their range. Thanks also to Jack Berkovi whose assistance with Chapter 2 was most useful, and Ros Baynes, of Management Pocketbook; who allowed me to extend some of the ideas originally produced for *The Meetings Pocketbook*. In addition, special thanks are due to my contacts at Pitman Publishing (who published my earlier book *Marketing for Non-Marketing Managers* in this same series) and who have consistently been a help and support. Incidentally, they will have noticed, I hope, that the manuscript for this book arrived *ahead* of the deadline – just.

Patrick Forsyth
Summer 1994

1

Time: a key resource
The opportunities and the difficulties

'Success is a process, a quality of mind and way of being, an outgoing affirmation of life'
ALEX NOBLE

Whatever job you do, if you are in a management or executive role, then you will utilise a number of resources. People, money, materials – all are important. In any particular job one or more of these, or others, may predominate. But there is one resource we all have in common: time. And time is a hard task master. Everyone experiences problems occasionally getting everything done that needs to be done, and doing it all in the time available. For some, such problems seem perpetually to exist to one degree or another; others will admit to having moments when things seem to conspire to prevent work going as planned, and a few to living in a state of permanent chaos.

So everyone can potentially benefit from reviewing how to manage their time effectively. Who needs to think about time management? In any organisation many of the things that actually characterise its very nature make proper time management difficult: hierarchical structures, people, deadlines, paperwork, meetings, pressures and interactions, both around the organisation and externally; all these and more can compound the problems. So, this book aims to help solve the problems of time management for all those working in executive or managerial positions within organisations, whether commercial or otherwise, and who are charged with getting things done and achieving results. If you are in this category, even if you have already made strenuous attempts to organise the way you work, then you may pick up ideas that will help you achieve more. If you see yourself as having too much to do, if you have too little time in which to do it, if coping with the urgent means you never get to all the important things on your list, and you would like to be more organised and do not quite know how to go about becoming so, then this book is directed at you. If your desk is piled with untidy heaps of paper, you are constantly subject to interruptions, your deadlines are impossible and you despair of ever being able to get your head above water, then this book is directed at you too. In fact if you are in the last category, then you may not be able to do without some sort of review of how you work.

Time management is not an option. It is something that everyone who wants to work effectively must consider, whether formally or informally. In fact, except for the rare person who works entirely at random, everyone practises time management to some degree; the only question is how well they do it and how it affects what they do. Yet time management is not easy — something you may well have noticed! Nor, even for those who work at it, is it something that anyone gets one hundred per cent right. If you think that is a rather ominous start to a book on time management, there is worse to come. In his book *What's Wrong with the World* the classic author G.K. Chesterton wrote: 'The Christian ideal has not been tried and found wanting. It has been found difficult; and left untried'. So it is also with time management. Just because it is difficult, the temptation can be to despair of ever making a real difference, and to give up on it, letting things take their course and muddling through somehow. To varying degrees this temptation is often very strong.

But, and it is a positive but, you *can* make a difference and such a difference can not only be worthwhile, it can have a radical effect on both job and career.

Make no mistake, the effects of getting to grips with time management can be considerable and varied. First, it can affect your efficiency, effectiveness and productivity. This alone makes your attitude to time management very important, for it affects your work day by day, hour by hour, all the time. Secondly, and as a consequence, it will condition the pressure that goes with any job. Further, there are other impacts. Of course, if you achieve more that is good. But it may also create greater positive visibility. Time management is something that will influence how you are perceived by others within the organisation. Good time management is an overriding factor that can act to differentiate people of otherwise equal talent and ability, making it more likely that some will succeed better in career terms than others. Therefore, although it may take some time, getting to grips with your own personal system of time management is immensely important.

Time management must be seen as synonymous with self management; it demands discipline, but a discipline that is reinforced by habit. In other words, the good news is that it gets easier as you work at it. Good habits help ensure that a well-organised approach is brought consistently to bear on the way you plan and executive your work. On the other hand, bad habits are difficult to shift. This is something you may have personally experienced if you have ever tackled, say, giving up smoking. And the changing of habits is something that may well be a necessary subsequence of any review of how you work.

Making time management work for you is based on two key factors: how you plan your time and how you implement the detail of what you do. The first of these, which is reviewed in the early part of this book, creates an important foundation upon which you can then build and work. The second consists of a multitude of operational factors, practices, methods and tricks, all of which can individually and positively affect the way in which you work. Such factors may be absurdly simple, for example, visibly checking your watch from time to time will tend to make visitors less likely to overstay their welcome, especially if such checks are accompanied by the appropriate look of concern. Or they may demand more complexity, for example, a well set-up filing system can save time in many ways, ensuring, for instance, that you can locate papers quickly and accurately. Then again other factors may be downright sneaky, like having a private signal to prompt your secretary to interrupt a meeting with news of something demanding its rapid curtailment or your prompt departure. What is more, there is a cumulative effect at work here. This means that the more you adopt or adapt the tricks of the trade, as it were, that work for you, the more time efficient you become. This is a process that most of us can continue to add to and work on throughout our career. So, unless you are a paragon of time efficient virtue, a review of whether you are working in the best possible way is nearly always worthwhile. Indeed, it can pay dividends to keep a regular eye on this throughout your working life. This too can become a habit.

A personal approach

Because of the way time management works, influenced as it is by many things, what works in any particular kind of job or for any particular individual will vary. Some of the ideas you will find presented here, or elsewhere, you will be able to add profitably to our own working habits. Some will be new to you; some you will know but may not be utilising effectively or to their full potential in terms of the assistance they can provide for you. Others will be able to form only the basis of what will suit you. They will need personalising, tailoring to the circumstances in which you work, and it is always important to consider this option with any idea you review before rejecting it. Be careful not to reject out of hand anything that might be useful in amended form; this is an area where every small influence can assist your overall productivity. Of course, still other ideas will not suit you at all. However much you tinker with them they will not form a useful basis for the kind of way in which you work. So be it. The aim should be to review thoroughly and then use every possible way to enhance the productivity of *your* job. What matters is arriving at a point at which you are content that having explored the possibilities for action, you have selected, adapted and experimented with all the methods that can realistically fit in with the way you work and assist your productivity. It is you that matters ultimately, not the principles. However, do remember that anything – but anything – that can help should be considered and, unless it has a negative impact, made part of your working practice. Good time management comes from leaving no stone unturned.

The productivity gain

Time is relative (thank you Mr. Einstein) and, as has been said, it is a resource as valuable as any other. Yet it is so easy to squander. Why is it that there is in most organisations a predisposition to focus thought and effort on the appropriate use of other resources, money for instance, and that the view of time is so often different? The sheer difficulty of some aspects of time management and the power of habit explain some of this, but there is, I think, another reason.

Those of a certain age will remember the ground-breaking revue Peter Cook and others brought to the London stage under the title *Beyond the Fringe*. One sketch was about the possibility of a nuclear war. In those days it was said that the early warning radar would give four minutes warning of any enemy missiles coming our way. 'What can you do in four minutes?' asked one character incredulously. 'Some people', came the reply, 'can run a mile in four minutes!' That may be, but it is still not a very long time, and would doubtless have been sadly inadequate for the task of escaping from an atomic bomb. But four minutes is still, well, four minutes, and it is an important principle of time management that even small periods of time can readily add up to a worthwhile amount.

Consider four minutes saved – by not running that mile perhaps. It is a short time and may not be immediately considered of very much practical use. However, if the four minutes is saved by increasing efficiency on one small task which is executed regularly then, for something done every day, that adds up to more than 14 hours over a year! That is very nearly as much as two working days, and should give anyone pause for thought. What could you do – extra – if you had two additional working days at your disposal? It is undeniably a useful amount of time and most people have probably got a dozen jobs on their list that could be got out of the way if such an additional two days were really available. This thought comes from imagining what speeding up just one small regular task or perhaps avoiding wasting time, to the tune of just four minutes can do for you. So, another significant reason why time management may be neglected is that the individual savings of time that it makes possible, or certainly some of them, seem unimportant. We tend to wonder what five minutes here or there matters, when what is really needed is a clear day – or even a clear hour – without interruptions. Yet clearly such short moments add up.

If this fact is recognised, and time and activities planned accordingly, then it is possible to free up considerable amounts of time. What is more, this can often be done at minimal cost. This is worth noting, as many potential improvements to efficiency do have a cost. If you want new equipment, more in your budget, more people, then in many organisations this takes some considerable justification. Sometimes such requests are seen as just a matter of your personal convienience and sometimes too, after all the requisitioning, the answer is simple; it is 'no'. But time is yours to utilise. It is an area where you can make a real difference to performance armed with little more than the intention to do so.

Speculate to accumulate

A further point needs stating before we turn to areas of individual action. You will find that some ways of saving time, or better utilising it, do need an investment – but it is an investment of time. It seems like a contradiction in terms, having to spend time to save time. Again this can all too easily become a barrier to action. Yet the principle is clear: there is a time equation that can and must be put to work if time is to be brought under control. There are many ways of ensuring that time is utilised to best effect, and, while some take only a moment, others take time either to set up or for you to adopt the habit of working in a particular way.

If we consider an example then the point becomes clear. This is linked to delegation, a subject we return to later and to the phrase you have perhaps said to yourself, or at any rate is oft repeated: 'It is quicker to do it myself'. When this thought comes to mind, sometimes, and certainly in the short term, the sentiment may well be correct. It *is quicker* to do it yourself. But beware, because this may only be true at the moment something occurs. Say someone telephones you requesting certain information, it does not matter what, but imagine that you must locate and look something up, compose a brief comment to explain it and send the information off to the other person with a note of the comment. It is a minor matter and will take you 3–4 minutes.

Imagine further that, to avoid the task, you consider letting your secretary do it. She is well able to, but explaining and showing her what needs to be done will certainly take 10–15 minutes of both your time and hers. It really is quicker to do it yourself. Not so. Or rather certainly not if it is a regularly occurring task. Say it is something that happens half a dozen times a week. If you take the time to brief your secretary then she will only have to take the action for less than a week and the time spent briefing will have paid off; thereafter you save a significant amount of time every week, indeed on every occasion that similar requests are made on into the future. This is surely worthwhile. The time equation here of time spent as a ratio of time saved works positively. This is often the case and worthwhile savings can be made by applying this principle, both to simple examples such as that just stated, or to more complex matters where hours or days spent on, say, reorganising a system or process may still pay dividends.

So why is it so difficult to take this sort of action? Why is the world full of managers and others all saying that it is quicker to do some things themselves? Some of the reasons in the example given above may be to do with attitudes to delegation (to which we return later), beyond that it is largely habit and lack of thought – and perhaps the pressure of the moment. We judge it is possible to pause from what we are presently doing for the few moments necessary to get another task out of the way, but not for longer in order to carry out a briefing that would rid us of the task altogether, and ultimately make a real time saving. It is worth a thought. Become determined not to be caught in this time trap and you are en route to saving a great deal of time.

Given the right intention, and motivation, it is possible for anyone to improve their time utilisation, and perhaps for those who have not given any aspect of time management much conscious thought of late to improve the way they work markedly. Make no mistake however, the process does not stop there. It takes more than a review of time management and the adoption to one or two ideas to make you truly productive for life. A review will kick start the process, but the right way of thinking must continue it. The best time managers have not only instilled in themselves good habits and so put part of the process on automatic pilot, as it were, they also view time management as an area of perpetual fine tuning. In everything they do the time dimension is considered. It becomes a prerequisite for the various ways in which they work, and they continuously strive to improve still further the way they work and what it allows them to achieve. That fine tuning too becomes a habit.

Perfect time

One final point needs making by way of introduction. Time management is very much an area where the old saying 'never let perfection be the enemy of the good' is entirely appropriate. However well you approach the management of your time, you are never going to be able to regard it as perfect. Nothing in the art of time management, nor reading this book, will guarantee that you will never not be able to find anything again, nor will it mean nothing takes longer in future than you think it will, nor that you are never interrupted again, not least at a crucial moment. Nor does it mean that you will never again find yourself saying: 'if only I had more time'. Indeed, in many management jobs there is a creative element. You are employed to make things happen, to innovate, review and change things and to do so in a dynamic environment where it sometimes seems that nothing stays the same for five whole minutes. It is inherent in such circumstances that there will always be new things to do and that, as a consequence, you will never get to the bottom of the 'things to do' list. The time to worry is not when you have too much to do, but more when you do not have sufficient to do.

But though perfection may not be possible, improvement certainly is. Every saving of time, every efficiency, whether large or small, adds to the total way in which your style of work contributes to your effectiveness. Any aspect of a job can probably be changed for the better, in terms of how it is done, so as to use time more productively. This means that the job is to actively organise what you do and how you do it to produce optimum working and make you really effective. It is this process that using the principles of time management and adopting the right attitude can assist. Doing this and doing it thoroughly will benefit your organisation and it will benefit you; and some of those benefits can come quickly.

First, however, you need to look at the way you work now, before turning your thinking to those ideas and practices that can assist it. It is to current practice that we turn to at the start of the second chapter. Meantime, Fig. 1.1 shows a version of the now ubiquitous 'Murphy's Laws'. Why these maxims should be accredited to Mr Murphy is long lost in the mists of time (perhaps it is because, being an Irish name, it links to a country with its own definition of time, and certainly with no local word meaning 'urgent', though it is, in part, the relaxed attitude to time that gives Ireland its considerable charm). However they came by their name, they can still raise a wry smile, though act also as a reminder of the less than perfect world in which time management must seek to have an effect.

1 If anything *can* go wrong, it *will* do so.

2 Nothing is *ever* as simple as it seems.

3 If you mess with something for long enough, it will break.

4 If you try to please everybody, somebody won't like it.

5 Nothing ever works out exactly as you expect.

6 Whatever you *want* to do, there is always something else you have to do first.

7 If you explain something so that no one could *possibly* misunderstand, someone will.

8 Nothing is certain until it has happened (and then you should check it more than once).

9 If everything is going according to plan, then it is a sure sign that something is about to go wrong.

10 The only predictable thing about your day is that something totally unexpected will happen.

Fig. 1.1 Murphy's Ten Laws of Time Management

You doubtless know the feeling conjured up by these 'laws' only too well. As was said earlier in this chapter, no one manages their time perfectly – not least because there are so many things conspiring to prevent it. But let us turn to practical issues and begin to see how we can move in the right direction.

Assessing your situation

First steps towards effective time management

'Whatever the right hand finds to do, the left hand carries a watch to show how long it takes to do it'

RALPH SOCKMON

There are many activities where the whole is greater than the sum of the individual parts. For instance, if you wanted to learn to juggle with flaming torches, there is more than the specific movements of the hands to study. Success in executing the trick will depend also on overall coordination, concentration *and* getting the individual movements exactly right. Only then will you avoid burning holes in the carpet. Time management is similar. The individual techniques, ideas and tricks of the trade will allow you to achieve some progress towards an effective and efficient way of working, but only approaching the process on a broad front will lead to a sustained overall way of working that will ensure continuing effectiveness. Unless the right attitude is brought to bear, then time management will only ever be a question of various techniques in danger of being adopted initially with enthusiasm but quickly being less rigorously applied.

Thus time management involves not just keeping your paperwork tidy and your desk clear, but a whole way of working that underlies all your actions and interfaces with all facets of your job. Because of this we review next a number of all-embracing rather than individual factors that need applying with an eye on the whole of the rest of your job and the range of tasks it entails. They start, logically enough, with the need to assess how you work now as a basis for considering action and possibly changes in the future.

The executive work mix

Whatever your individual job, whether you are manager or executive, and regardless of the type of organisation for which you work and the functional area in which you are involved, you have, in all probability, many different things to do. Too many perhaps. These are different in nature and complexity, and involve different time scales. They range across a thousand and one things, from drafting a letter or report to planning the relocation of the entire organisation to new offices or the launching of a new product. What is more, you probably have a good many things on the go at once and overlapping, and maybe conflicting, priorities. Often work feels just like the juggling analogy referred to above, and your 'reach' – how much you can keep on the go at once – is an important aspect of your effectiveness. If you exceed your reach then, like the juggler, the danger is that you do not simply drop one torch but several.

It helps the consideration of managing all of this effectively to categorise the many elements. There are doubtless many ways of doing this, but for our purposes four categories seem to bring some order to the picture:

(i) *Planning*: this is the prerequisite to all action. Many tasks are involved: research, investigation, analysis and testing amongst others. This area may also involve consultation and ultimately the communication of plans and is, of course, the key to decision making.

(ii) *Implementation*: simply stated, doing things – of all sorts – whether intangible, of which the key one is making decisions, or tangible. Specific tasks divide importantly into two sorts, first *individual tasks*. These are free standing. They may be major or minor, for example, a writing task may entail composing a two-line memo or a 20-page report (or a book). Secondly, progressing tasks where a series of actions are closely linked and contribute cumulatively to achieving an overall end result. Moving offices, referred to above, would involve such action and such things may be more clearly visualised rather than described – indeed this is a useful and time efficient way of working on them. Fig. 2.1 shows a typical progressing task and illustrates the interrelationship of the various actions. Tasks in both categories may well need to be linked to planning activity on whatever scale.

ASSESSING YOUR SITUATION

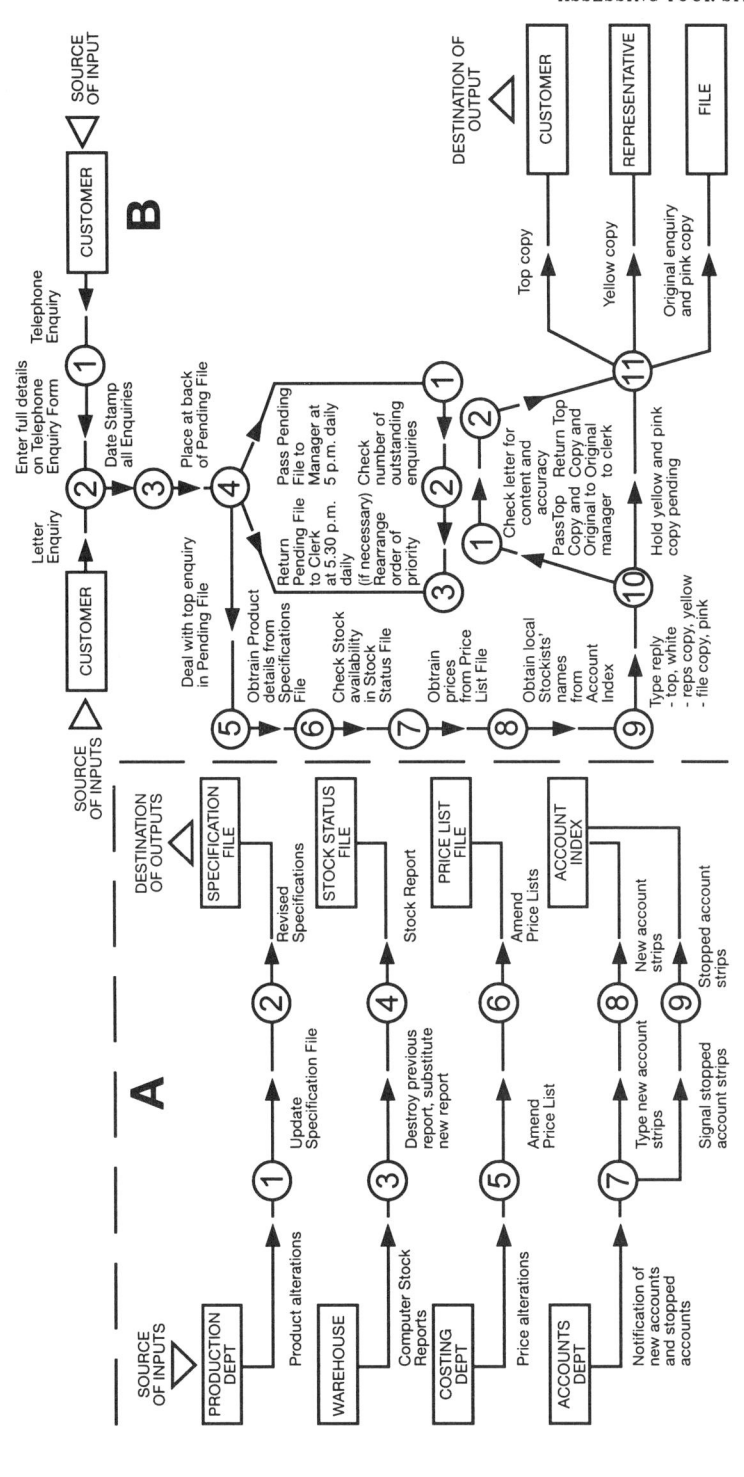

NETWORK ANALYSIS AND FLOW CHART FOR ANSWERING CUSTOMER ENQUIRIES AND UPDATING INFORMATION FILES

This figure was originated for me to augment some course material by David Collischon, who wrote the Foreword to this book, and originally appeared in my book *Running an Effective Sales Office* (now in its second edition as a Gower paperback).

Fig. 2.1 Progressing tasks: example

11

(iii) *Monitoring and control*: whatever is done may need checking to ensure it is being done in the best possible way and bringing the desired results. Checking may be simple, editing the draft of a report or running it through the word processor's spelling checker for example. Or it may be complex, as are many financial control systems.

(iv) *Communicating and dealing with people*: this clearly overlaps with the other three categories of activity, but is inherent to the work of almost everyone. Take the people out of an organisation and there is nothing meaningful left. Few, if any, people work in isolation from others, and for most the people issues, whether it is briefing them or reporting to them, meetings and other forms of communication with them, are an essential part of their work and take up a major part of their time.

In all four categories above there will, or should be, a strong link with objectives and achievement of results. All tasks, all action should focus on the overall aims and are often of little significance in themselves. Effectiveness is measured ultimately by achievement. Time management must not be seen as only concerned with packing more activity into the available time, though this may be part of it, it must be instrumental in assisting to ensure objectives are met. It may be a cliché, but it must never be forgotten that activity must never be confused with achievement.

With this picture in mind we can look specifically at current working practice.

Assessing your current working practice

You may think that you know how you work; perhaps you feel you know all too well how you work – warts and all. But do not be misled into thinking that considering the detail of this is a waste of time. Classically, improving anything implies the identification of how it is now. This gives a measure against which to judge how we might progress. Further, such an analysis can provide valuable information about where the greatest improvement may be found, all of which makes improvement more likely. This is certainly true of time management, more so perhaps because this is an area where there is a real tendency to self delusion. If I ask if you spend too much time in meetings, you may well agree. But do you waste time doing unnecessary paperwork? Do you spend too much time socialising? Are you badly organised? Such questions are more likely to put most people on the defensive, and understandably so. You are no doubt essentially efficient, but improvement may still be possible. Indeed, most people would value more time to complete their tasks and undertake their responsibilities, if this were possible; for most, it is.

To make other than superficial changes, you need to know something about your own working practices and pressures, and where time goes at present (this last we turn to in the next paragraph). In a complex job many activities are involved. The questions in Fig. 2.2 provide a systematic way of taking your time management temperature. Have a look at them, follow the instructions accompanying them and you will see how you rate currently. Remember, if your rating is less than perfect, that perfection is not attainable and that there will be many pressures creating the picture you see, some self inflicted, others not; and many such pressures may be changeable.

Study the questions in Fig. 2 overleaf and mark your immediate response to them in terms of whether you strongly agree (SA), mildly agree (MA), mildly disagree (MD) or strongly disagree (SD). Then see the note which follows the list of questions.

	SA	MA	MD	SD
1 I regularly need more time to finish my key tasks.				
2 I regularly take work home from the office.				
3 I prepare a daily list of things to do.				
4 I seem to have very little time to myself at work.				
5 My boss often asks me to do tasks at short notice.				
6 I spend a lot of time in meetings.				
7 I like to complete the simple, quick tasks early in the day to allow time later for the larger tasks.				
8 I have difficulty in starting a large, complex task or project.				
9 I have to arrive at the office early or work late to get my job done.				
10 I spend a lot of my work time travelling.				
11 I often have to deal with crises in my department.				
12 I always set myself daily work goals.				
13 I deal with my mail when it arrives.				
14 I often have difficulty in finishing a large task.				
15 I like to get involved in the detail of a project to ensure that it is done correctly.				
16 My boss meets with me regularly to review progress on key tasks.				
17 A lot of my time is wasted during meetings.				
18 I regularly list the tasks which need to be done.				
19 I enjoy taking on more tasks when asked.				
20 I have a copy of my boss's job objectives.				
21 My desk or work area is rather cluttered and could be neater.				
22 I need more reading time to keep up with issues related to my work.				

Fig. 2.2 **Personal time management profile**

ASSESSING YOUR SITUATION

	SA	MA	MD	SD
23 I spend a lot of time on paperwork.				
24 I don't have enough time for family, friends or other important non-work activities.				
25 I often need an approaching deadline to make me start a difficult or large task.				
26 I find it easier and quicker to do things myself rather than ask someone else.				
27 My working day often starts with reading newspapers, conversation or coffee/tea.				
28 Interruptions take up a lot of my time at work.				
29 I spend a lot of time searching for information related to my work.				
30 I tend to put off unpleasant tasks.				
31 I have a problem handling stress, tension or anxiety.				
32 I often forget to follow up or check on tasks I have delegated.				
33 I receive a lot of 'drop-in' visitors at work.				
34 I am involved in too many details, and tend to create bottlenecks or slow down the work of my staff or others.				
35 I often feel that my meetings could accomplish more.				
36 I enjoy working long hours.				
37 I often move from task to task and leave things unfinished.				
38 I can find quiet, uninterrupted time when I need it.				
39 I have a training plan for myself and my people.				
40 I meet regularly with my staff to discuss their progress on key tasks.				
41 After some meetings I am not always sure of what is expected of me.				
42 I often miss important deadlines.				
43 I take work home at weekends.				

Fig. 2.2 cont'd

	SA	MA	MD	SD
44 Some tasks take a lot longer than I thought they would and I often end up tackling too much at once.				
45 I often take less than my full holiday allocation.				
46 I like to change and develop new habits.				
47 I expect my people to work long hours.				
48 My filing system could be improved.				
49 Meetings I call start on time, stay on time and end on time.				
50 Changing priorities keep me from completing my workload.				

Fig. 2.2 cont'd

There are no right or wrong answers. Sometimes agreement indicates current effectiveness, sometimes the reverse. The list of factors below shows how these kinds of detail from the way in which you work group into areas that need attention in time management terms, all are areas of potential improvement – as we will see.

Job purpose (questions 1, 20, 37, 39, 41, 49)
A number of profile questions relate to whether you have an ability to focus your energy and activities. These examine clarification of job objectives, focus on results and why you spend your time in a particular way.

Job patterns (questions 4, 9, 12, 13, 15, 36, 46)
We often spend a great deal of our time on routines. Time log analysis will reveal your actual time usage. These profile questions reveal whether you had a knowledge beforehand of any patterns in your job and whether there is a gap between your activities and desired results.

Procrastination (questions 7, 8, 14, 30, 37)
These questions refer to your ability to avoid unnecessary delay in starting and completing important work, and how you act in various situations. We often prefer to do the easy things first, but these may not be the most important.

Job planning (questions 3, 18, 22, 25, 32, 38, 42, 44, 50)
These questions relate to the way you structure your working day towards achieving your desired results, how you monitor what is happening and your efforts to control your tasks and time spent.

Time wasters (questions 17, 21, 27, 28, 33, 35, 41)
Many time wasters occur during the working day which upset our plans and lower our expected performance. The profile reveals how well you handle such situations.

People (questions 5, 6, 11, 16, 26, 31, 34, 40, 47)
These questions reveal your co-operative approach when people are involved with your workload. We have to work with other people and sometimes conflicts of priorities occur. We often think that other people cause our poor performance; however, good time management recognises that *we* are often part of the poor performance problem.

Paperwork (questions 23, 29, 48)
Most of your work involves some level of detail and information flow, generally paper-based. This part of the profile examines how well you 'move' your paperwork rather than let it pile up.

Personal (questions 2, 10, 19, 24, 31, 43, 45)

This part of the profile reveals how your personal characteristics affect the way your time is spent, and addresses the necessary balance between work and non-work activity.

(This Profile material was developed by Jack Berkovi for course material used by the Marketing Improvements Group to whom I am grateful for permission to reproduce this here.)

Having considered these questions and how your answers cumulatively begin to give a rounded picture of how you approach your work (and some of the habits involved), you can logically move on to consider how your time is split currently across the variety of work you undertake.

Where times goes now

There are two ways to do this. The first is to estimate it, guesstimate it might be a better phrase; this is most easily done in percentage terms on a pie chart (see Fig. 2.3). The second is to use a time log to obtain a much more accurate picture – literally recording what you do through the day and doing so for at least a week, longer if you can (the chore of noting things down takes only a few seconds, but must be done punctiliously). This is shown in Fig. 2.4.

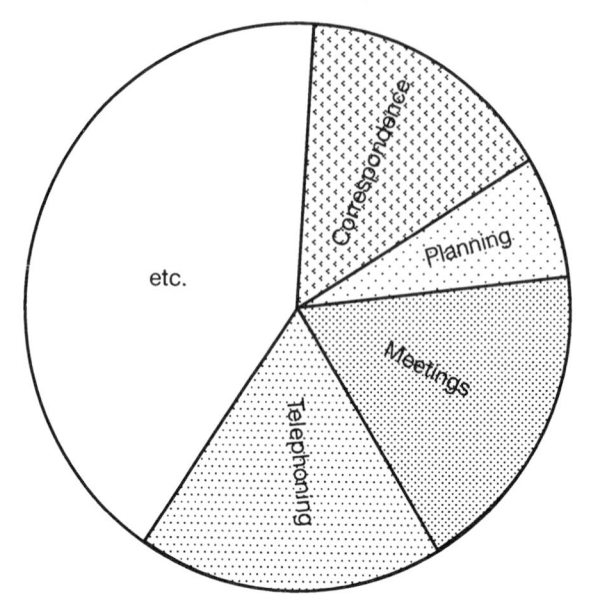

Fig. 2.3 Assess where your time goes now

Few, if any, people keep a log without surprising themselves, and the surprises can be either that much more time is spent in some areas than you think, or that certain things take up less time than you think – mainly the former. Some obvious areas for review tend to come to mind as a result.

Again using the simple pie chart, it can be useful as a second stage of this review to list what you would ideally like the time breakdown to be. This puts a clear picture in your mind of what you are working towards. Such a picture might even be worth setting out before you read on.

All this gives you something to aim towards and will tell you progressively – as you take action – whether that action is having a positive effect. If all the remaining review points are looked at alongside this information then you can see more clearly whether you are able to take action to improve things, and whether the points refer to areas that are critical for you.

ASSESSING YOUR SITUATION

Name:	Comments:
Date:	

No.	Start time	Activity description	Time Taken (minutes)	Priority* category				Comments
				A	B	C	D	
1								
2								
3								
4								
5								
6								
7								
8								
9								
10								
11								
12								
13								
14								
15								
16								
17								
18								
19								
20								
21								
22								
23								

Total time taken (minutes):

* Link these columns to any priority code *you* use

Fig. 2.4 Personal time performance log (example)

With all this in mind, we turn to what is both one of the basics of time management and perhaps its most practically important tenet.

The necessity for a clear plan

There is a wise saying that you should 'plan the work, and work the plan'. Certainly any real progress with time management needs a plan. This must be in writing and must be reviewed and updated regularly; for most people this means a daily check.

I repeat: a *written* plan and a *regular* check and update.

It is thus what is sometimes called a rolling plan, not only is it updated regularly, it provides a snapshot of your workload ahead at any particular moment. As such it should show accurately and completely your work plan for the immediate future, and give an idea of what lies beyond. As you look ahead there will be some things that are clear a long way ahead, for example, when an annual budget must be prepared and submitted, other areas are less clear and, of course, much cannot be anticipated at all in advance.

At its simplest such a plan is just a list of things to do. It may include:

- a daily plan
- a weekly plan
- commitments that occur regularly (weekly or monthly or annually)
- a plan for the coming month (perhaps linked to a planning chart)

The exact configuration will depend on the time span across which you work. What is important is that it works for you, that it is clear, that different kinds of activity show up for what they are and that it links clearly to your diary and appointment system. How such a list is arranged and how you can use it to improve your work and effectiveness form part of the content of this book, but the fact of the system and the thinking that its regular review prompts is important in its own right. It is the basic factor in creating a time management discipline, and it provides much of the information from which you must make choices – what you do, delegate, delay or ignore, in what order you tackle things and so on. Good time management does not remove the need to make decisions of this sort, but it should make them easier and quicker to make and it should enable you to make decisions which really do help in a positive way, so that you get

ASSESSING YOUR SITUATION

more done and in the best way in terms of achieving your aims.

If this is already beginning to sound like hard work, do not despair. I do not believe that the process of updating and monitoring your rolling plan will itself become an onerous task. It will vary a little day by day, and is affected by your work pattern, but on average it is likely to take only a few minutes. I reckon I keep a good many balls in the air and am a busy person; my own paperwork on this takes perhaps five minutes a day, but – importantly – this prevents more time being taken up in less organised juggling during the day.

A final point here is crucial. Some people, perhaps most, have a measure of their day which is reactive. Things occur which cannot be predicted, at least individually, and a proportion of the available time is always going to go in this way. Such activity is not automatically unimportant, and the reverse may well be true. For example, a manager on the sales or marketing side of a commercial company may have enquiries and queries coming from customers which are very important and must be dealt with promptly, but will nevertheless make fitting in everything else more difficult. Sometimes the reaction to this is to believe that, because of this reactive element, it is not possible to plan or to plan effectively. The reverse is true. If your days do consist even in part of this sort of random activity, it is even more important to plan because there is inherently less time available to do the other things that the job involves and that time has to be planned even more thoroughly to maximise its effectiveness (see Fig. 2.5 reproduced from *Running an Effective Sales Office,* Patrick Forsyth, Gower).

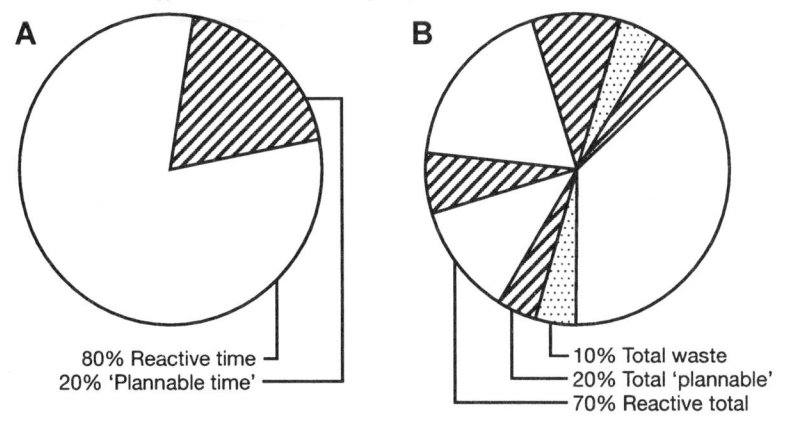

A
80% Reactive time
20% 'Plannable time'

B
10% Total waste
20% Total 'plannable'
70% Reactive total

Note: More likely as in B the 'plannable', ▨ time will occur at random throughout our day. Add an amount for an element of wasted time ⊡.

Fig. 2.5 Planning limited 'plannable time'

Everyone needs a plan, everyone can benefit from having a clear view of what there is to be done. If you do not have this then the work of setting it up will take a moment, but it is worthwhile and, as has been said, it need not then take long to keep up to date. Once it is in place, you can evolve a system that suits you and that keeps up with the way in which your job and its responsibilities change over time.

So far I have ignored the question of what paperwork is needed to implement this planning process. It is worth noting that many books on the subject of time management are closely linked to some specific proprietary time management system, consisting of diaries, files, binders and in some cases more besides. Some even claim that the only route to time efficiency lies with the particular system they recommend. Now this may be fine if the system suits you, but I would suggest caution in taking up any particular system.

This book is not linked in this way, and will recommend no one system; I do not in fact use such a branded system myself. This is not to say that I disapprove of them. One of the most organised people I know uses one and swears by it; but I also know people who are the very opposite of organised and yet whose desks are adorned with the binders and card indices of their chosen system, so they certainly offer no kind of panacea. Many are restrictive, that is they can only be used in a particular way and that may well not suit you and the way you think and work. There is thus a real danger that if you use a system and some element of it does not work for you, then your use of the whole system falters.

A better way is perhaps to work out what you need first: what kind of diary, how much space for notes, how many sections to fit the way your tasks are grouped, what permanent filing. Then, when you have thought through what you need and worked that way for a while (a process which will almost certainly have you making a few changes in the light of how things actually work), you can check out the systems and see whether any of them formalise what you want to do and, as they can be expensive, make the investment in one worthwhile. Otherwise the world is full of people who organise themselves perfectly well with no more than a diary, a notebook or a file. To end with something of a recommendation, I would suggest a loose-leaf diary system is a good basis for many (I use a desk-sized Filofax). This combines a neat system with the flexibility to put in exactly what *you* need, and that is what is most important. After all, it must reflect *your* plan and it is *your* time which you want to organise.

This recommendation is expanded in the Appendix (page 163) in which a number of Filofax forms are reproduced by way of example. At this stage the boxed illustration (Fig. 2.6) sets out an example of the components that might be used to implement whatever system you need and comments on some of the ways in which the inherent flexibility can work. I repeat, there is surely no one system that is right for everyone. Even the precise kind of diary layout you choose must be a personal decision based on your needs, and what else is necessary will reflect the way you work. You must decide; I can only state that all my experience suggests that a flexible and thus tailor-made system is likely to be best. Some of the items shown and the points made in Fig. 2.6 are investigated further as you read on.

Setting clear objectives

Any plan is, in turn, as good as the objectives that lie behind it. So it is to objectives, certainly a fundamental factor affecting the management of time, which is what this chapter promised to address, that we now turn. Clear objectives (the boxed paragraph defines what this means further) really are important, and any lack of clarity can affect every aspect of a person's work, not least time management, sometimes doing so surreptitiously.

Much of what needs to be done to manage time effectively is concerned with tackling conflicts and making decisions about what comes first, and none of this is possible if there is no underlying clarity about objectives to act as a reference.

This is not the place for a long treatise on objective setting, suffice it to say that this is important to everything in corporate life. A company functions best with clear corporate objectives, the management structure works best when individual managers are clear about what it is they are expected to achieve and, in turn, they can get the best out of their staff if they provide clear objectives for them. Consider your own position. Are there any areas that are not clear in this respect? If so, do they make for problems or conflict regarding the way you go about the job? If you answered 'yes' to the first question, then you probably did the same for the second.

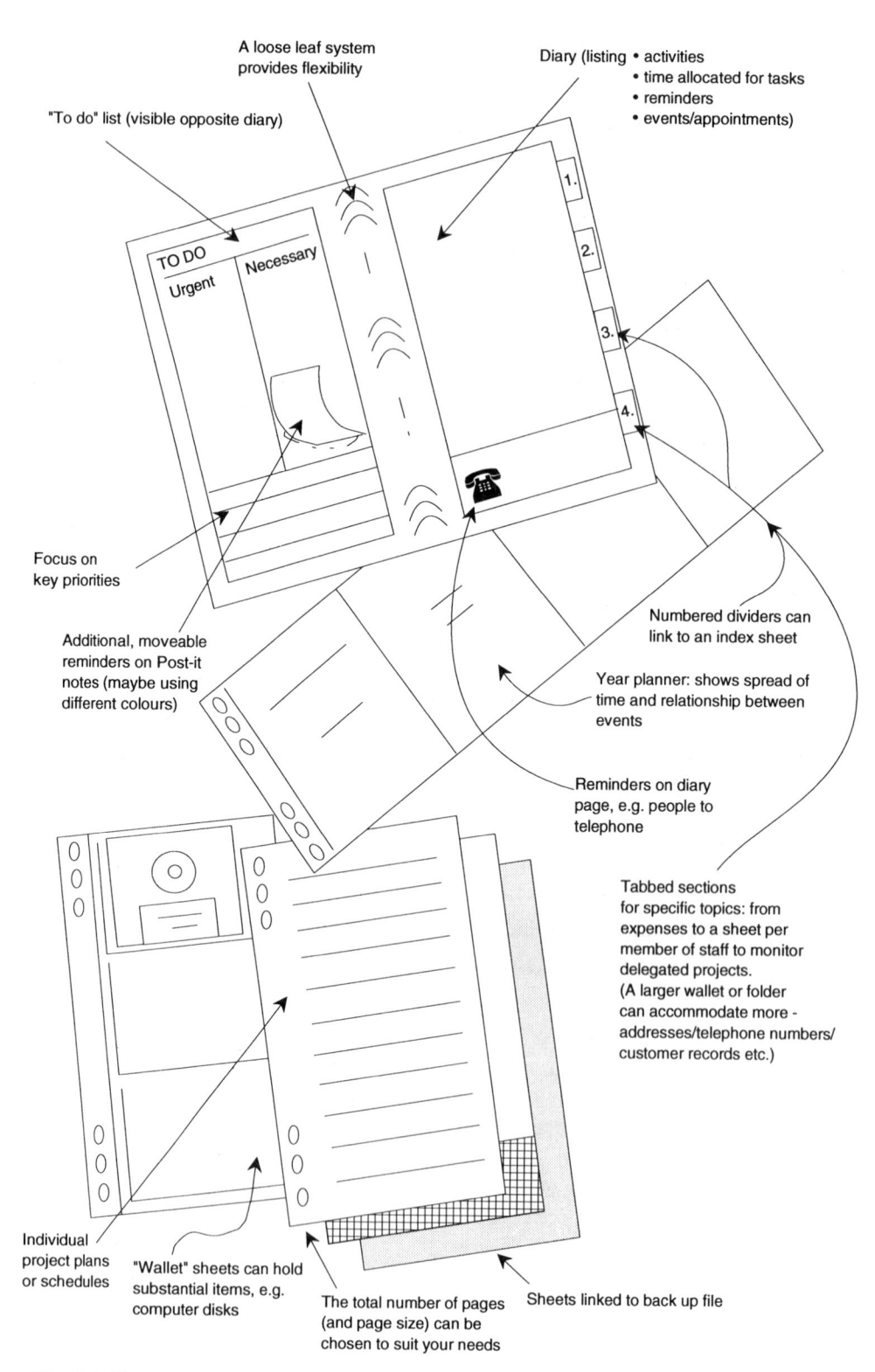

Fig. 2.6 Key components for planning your time

SETTING OBJECTIVES

Maxims advocating setting clear objectives are everywhere, and go back quite a while (see my favourite quotation on this topic below). It is sound advice; you *do* need clear objectives, and they must not be vague or general hopes.

A much quoted acronym spells out the principles involved: objectives should be SMART, that is: *Specific*, *Measurable*, *Achievable*, *Realistic*, and *Timed*. An example will help make this clear. A perennial area of management skill, on which I regularly conduct training, is that body of skills necessary in making formal presentations. (Incidentally, this too is an area with a link to time management. Any weakness in this area will tend to result in longer, and perhaps more agonising, preparation. Good presentation skills save time. But I digress, back to objectives.)

It is all too easy to define the objectives for a workshop on this topic as being simply to ensure participants 'make better presentations', a statement that is unlikely to be sufficiently clear to be really useful. Applying the formula might produce a statement such as:

Objectives for a presentation skills course

- *Specific*
  To enable participants to make future presentations in a manner and style which will be seen as appropriate by their respective audiences, and which will enhance the message they put over.

- *Measurable*
  In other words, how will we know this has been achieved? Ultimately, in this case by the results of future presentations; but we might also consider that the trainer or the group, or both, will be able to judge this to a degree at the end of the event by observing the standard during practice.

- *Achievable*
  Can this be done? The answer in this case will depend on the prevailing standard before the course. If the people are inexperienced and their standard of presentation is low, then the answer may be that it cannot. If, as we assume for the sake of our developing example, they are people who are sufficiently senior, experienced and with some practice in the area of presentations, then the objectives should be achievable – given a suitable amount of time and a suitable programme.

- *Realistic*
  Picking up the last point, if the time, say, is inadequate then the objectives may not be realistic. These people can potentially be improved we might say, but not in one short session.

- *Timed*
  Timed in training terms will reflect the timing of the course; it may be

scheduled to take place in one month's time, so the objectives cannot, by definition, be realised before then. Also the duration: is a one, two or any other number of days programme going to do the job?

(This example is reproduced from *Running an Effective Training Session,* Patrick Forsyth, Gower Publishing)

Such an approach is far more likely to provide guidance in the form of clear objectives.

> 'Would you tell me, please, which way I ought to walk from here?'
> 'That depends a good deal on where you want to get to,' said the Cat.
> 'I don't much care where . . .' said Alice.
> 'Then it doesn't matter which way you walk,' said the Cat.
> 'So long as I get *somewhere*,' Alice added, as an explanation.
> 'Oh, you're sure to do that,' said the Cat, 'if you only walk long enough.'
> *Alice's Adventures in Wonderland,* LEWIS CARROLL

Even a simple example makes the point. If a manager is asked to review a system of some sort, it might be for many reasons: to improve accuracy, to speed up operations, to save money, or all three. But undertaking this task is going to take longer if any of this is unclear. Either time needs to be spent working out or checking objectives, or work is put in towards some arbitrary objective which proves inadequate; both end up taking up more time. So it is with one task and with the job overall. If you do not have a clear job description, or if you are uncertain what objectives you should be aiming towards, then check, seek clarification and managing what you do will at once be easier.

At this point we can take stock for a moment as some of the key issues are on the table. If you have an idea of where times goes now and how you really approach things, if you have a (written) plan – one that relates to the clear objectives for your job – then you can get to work with some hopes of being reasonably productive. But there are many factors that can work to increase that productivity. Some are not only fundamental, they are also good examples of the way in which approaches (ultimately habits) can exert a considerable and ongoing influence on your working practices. The rest of this chapter looks at several such issues; all are potentially of great value to the manager wanting to become truly time efficient.

Thinking ahead

This might appropriately be called the opposite of the 'if only . . .' school of ineffective time management. Too often managers find themselves in a crisis to which the resolution would be all too easy if we could wind the clocks back. 'If only we had done so and so earlier' we say as we contemplate a messy and time consuming process of unscrambling. In all honesty, though the unexpected can happen sometimes, crisis management is all too common, and often all too unnecessary. Coping well with crises that are, for whatever reason, upon us saves time; certainly if the alternative is panic. The boxed paragraph on page 28 makes some comments on coping with crisis.

If things are left late or ill thought out (and the two can often go together), then time is used up in a hasty attempt to sort things out at short notice. This tends to make any task more difficult and is compounded by whatever day-to-day responsibilities are current at the time. If you can acquire the habit of thinking ahead, and a system, as referred to above, will help you do this, then you are that much more likely to see when a start really needs to be made on something.

Some people find that to 'see' the pattern of future work and tasks in their mind's eye is difficult. One invaluable aid to this is the planning or wall chart. This enables you to create a picture of activities, and the time spans are very much clearer as you scan such a chart than when flicking through the pages of a diary. Charts come in all shapes and sizes; some are for the current year and are, effectively, large diaries, others are ruled for specific tasks and others still are designed for you to create the detail. The large ones come with a variety of stickers to help highlight what is important; some are even magnetic and can provide a permanently updatable guide to your schedule.

Whatever you do to document things, however, the key is to get into the habit of thinking ahead – at the same time and without disrupting the current day's workload. Anticipating problems and spotting opportunities can make a real difference to the way you work in the short term.

DON'T PANIC

Whatever the cause and implications of any crisis situation, and they may be wide and many, the rule has to be never to treat a crisis like a crisis. Panic implies an absence of all the usual management processes which are no less needed at such a time; perhaps they are needed in fuller measure than usual. Having a systematic approach in mind (and acquiring the habit of referring to it, albeit mentally) as a first conscious step to avoiding panic is useful. Blind unthinking action will rarely have the precision required to rescue the situation and more damage may be done – and more time wasted – as further, second stage action becomes necessary.

So, the rules are:

- stay cool and do not panic
- think (and what is more, take sufficient time to think straight)
- consider the full range of management skills that can be brought to bear to sort the situation out (this may include such simple tactics as delegating certain straightforward actions to give you time to resolve more complex issues, and more radical solutions, such as reviewing policy)
- make an action plan (especially important if there is any degree of complexity involved)
- consider the control aspect of that ongoing action plan (simplistically creating a mechanism to show progress and let you know when the crisis is past)

Then action can flow on a considered basis to systematically sort out the problem, at least as best as can be done – you cannot wind the clock back. And finally, attention can turn not only to the lessons to be learned (you want to be sure to avoid a repeat of the same or similar circumstances) but also to anything positive that might come from the whole incident.

A colleague with whom I work on an associate basis from time to time has an attractive poster in her office consisting of the Chinese characters meaning crisis. In fact it consists of two characters: the first meaning 'severe danger', the second meaning 'opportunity'. Enough said.

Thereafter, you need to keep things in proportion. A crisis may impose stresses and strains, and surviving the occasional one is part of most jobs – though working so that they do not occur is perhaps even more important – and there are stresses and strains without the crises:

'Any idiot can face a crisis – it's the day to day living that wears you out.'
ANTON CHEKHOV

Spend time to save time

Whatever actions you might consider to keep yourself well organised – and I hope this book will demonstrate that there are many such areas – they tend to fall into two categories. Either they are simple to implement and only take a moment, or they inherently take some time to set up, and perhaps thereafter some time also to acquire as a retained working habit. If you limit yourself to the former you will never maximise your time management effectiveness. So, I make no excuse for returning to an example, linked to delegation (to which we return in Chapter 7), used in Chapter 1. To recap: consider how often you have heard people say, 'It is quicker to do it myself'? Many times probably, and in the short term the sentiment is often correct. It *is quicker* to do it yourself, but this is only true at the moment something occurs. Say someone telephones you asking for some information, it does not matter what, but imagine that you must look something up, put a note with it and send it off with a personalised note or memo. If it is a common occurrence, you could show your secretary where to find the information and the kind of way it should be dealt with and then she could cope with it. But the explanation will take 10–15 minutes and you can do it yourself in 3–4 minutes. It really is quicker to do it yourself. Not so.

If you only take the time to explain, then the question only needs to be asked and your secretary take the action three or four times and the time spent briefing her will have paid off. Thereafter you are saving time on every occasion it happens and, what is more, if it happens regularly this time can quickly add up to something really worthwhile. Why is it so difficult to find and invest that initial 10–15 minutes to achieve this sort of thing? The reasons are the same on the simple scale exampled here as for much more complex matters. Some of the reasons in the example are to do with what needs to be done, delegation, and we will leave that until delegation is dealt with specifically in Chapter 7. Beyond that it is largely habit and lack of thought; and perhaps the pressure of the moment. It is possible to pause in what we are doing to do something else for five minutes, but not, we judge, to delay it more to fit in the discussion that would delegate the task.

The principle here stands some thought. If you can become determined not to be caught in the trap implicit here, then you are on a track which will save you a great deal of time in future. This leads to another view of time which many consider equally important.

FIRST THINGS FIRST

Taking time to think

There is a good training film on aspects of time management (*Time to Think*, Longman Training*). At the end of the film the main character, a manager who has come to grips with managing his time better, is sitting in his office. A colleague comes into the outer office and begins to walk past the secretary to see him. She stops him, says her manager is busy and suggests he makes an appointment to see him later. He looks past her at the manager sitting in his office (he is visible through a glass partition) and says: 'But he's not doing anything'. Immediately the secretary replies that: 'He's thinking; now do you want to see him this afternoon or . . .'. This incident makes a good point.

As a general rule it is true to say that the higher up the hierarchy of an organisation you go, the more time you are expected to spend thinking, planning and decision making and the less doing other things. It is also often true that the thinking, the planning and idea generation that goes into a job is usually one of the most important things to be done in that job. This is shown graphically in Fig. 2.7.

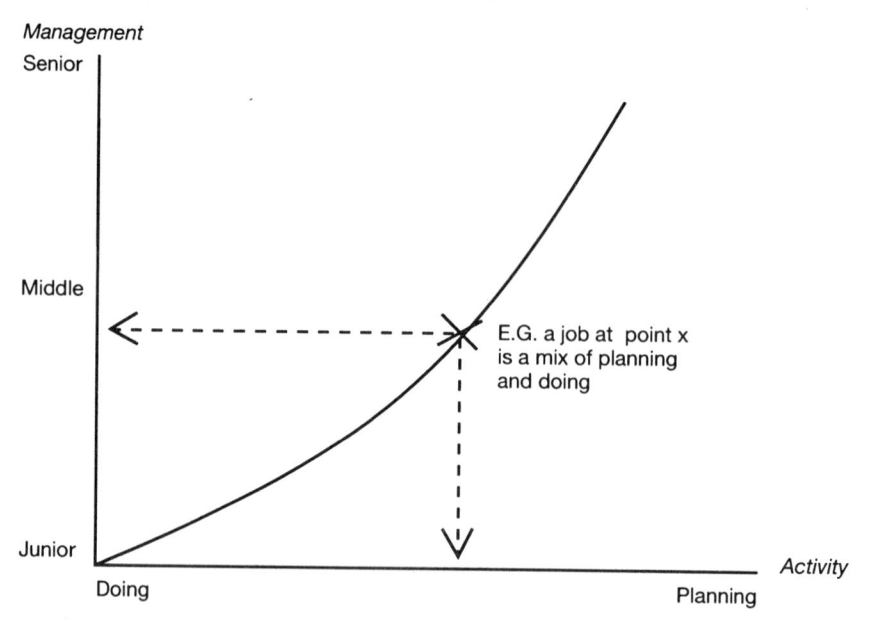

Fig. 2.7 The 'thinking/doing' mix

*Longman Training is one of the leading UK training resource companies and this film can be rented (or purchased, from them at: Longman House, Burnt Mill, Harlow, Essex.

And what is the most difficult kind of time to keep clear and have sufficient of'? Time to think will rank high. The moral is clear, one of the most important things your time management practices have to do is to make room for the thinking and creative time your job needs. Go back to your analysis of your time, or better still your time log if you did one (if not you should) and see how these activities show up. Are they getting the time they need and deserve or are they squeezed out by other pressures and what is more obviously urgent? I suggested earlier using the breakdown of your time and tasks (the pie chart in Fig. 2.3) as a guide for a more ideal breakdown. Make sure that you set your sights on sufficient thinking time – perhaps above all – and that the action you take to achieve this is not offset by the crises that all too easily beset any organisation or department. Without something approaching the ideal in this area all your objectives may be in jeopardy.

Be prepared to say 'no'

This is very much a first principle, and it needs some resolve to carry it through, so it is as well to have it in mind throughout your reading of the remainder of this book.

Everyone has to accept that they cannot do everything. This must probably be taken literally because there may be an almost infinite amount to do in any job that has some kind of inherent innovative or creative nature to it. Many people could just go on listing more and more things to do, not all equally important but deserving of a place on their 'to do' list nevertheless. Even if your job is not like this, you certainly have to accept that you are not going to do everything at the time you want. Both in terms of quantity and priority you are going to have to say 'no' to some things.

It is worth considering here not so much what you leave out but who you say 'no' to. For instance you may have to turn down:

- *colleagues*: what is involved here can vary and if there is a network of favours, with everyone helping everyone else, you do not want to let it get out of hand either way. Turn down too much and you end up losing time because people are reluctant to help you. Do everything unquestioningly and you may be seen as a soft touch and will end up doing more than your share. So balance is the keynote here, and timing; you do not have to do everything that crops up in this way instantly.

- *subordinates*: here they cannot tell you to do things, and while they need support, this must not get out of hand.
- *your own boss*: working with a boss who does not have enough to do, or who expects everything done instantly just because he is the boss, can play havoc with the best intentions of time management. You may need to regard it as your mission to educate them and need to conduct a campaign of persuasion and negotiation to keep any unreasonable load down.

With all of these you need to resolve to think before you agree, and to turn down involvements in some things even though they would be attractive to you. But this is not all; the most difficult person to say 'no' to may well be yourself. There are always many reasons for saying 'yes' to things: you do not wish to offend others, you *want* to do whatever it is, you do not think about the way a new thing impinges on the current workload etc. We all have our weak points in this regard. I remember being asked to speak at a conference. I was flattered to be asked, it was an important event, a topic I thought I was well qualified to tackle, so I wanted to do it. I looked up my diary whilst talking to the person who had called me on the telephone about it, and found the week concerned was very full, so was the period leading up to the date in question. But as my mind said it was just not on, my mouth said: 'I should be pleased to accept'. Such a story may put you in mind of similar situations you have faced. Beware of your own tendencies where they lead you away from priorities and resolve to be firm with others. Saying 'no' is a fundamental time saver. It was well put by Charles Spurgeon:

> 'Learn to say no; it will be more use to you than to be able to read Latin'

To be, or not to be (perfect)

Most people in a job they care about want to do things well (if you were not in that category you would probably not have picked up this book, much less persevered to this point; but I digress – and am in danger of wasting your time!). Some people take this further and are perfectionists. Now there is a place for this, and I would certainly not advocate that anyone adopts a shoddy approach to their work, whatever it may be. There is, however, a dichotomy here, one well summed up in a quotation from Robert Heimleur, who said (perhaps in some despair): 'They didn't want it good, they wanted it on Wednesday'. The fact is it takes time to achieve perfection, and in any case perfection may not always be strictly necessary. Things may need to be undertaken carefully, thoroughly, comprehensively, but we may not need to spend time getting every tiny detail perfect. This comes hard to those who are naturally perfectionists, and it is a trait that many have at least about some things, but it is necessary to strike a balance. Figure 2.8 shows graphically the balance to be struck between quality – the standard to which things are done – cost and time.

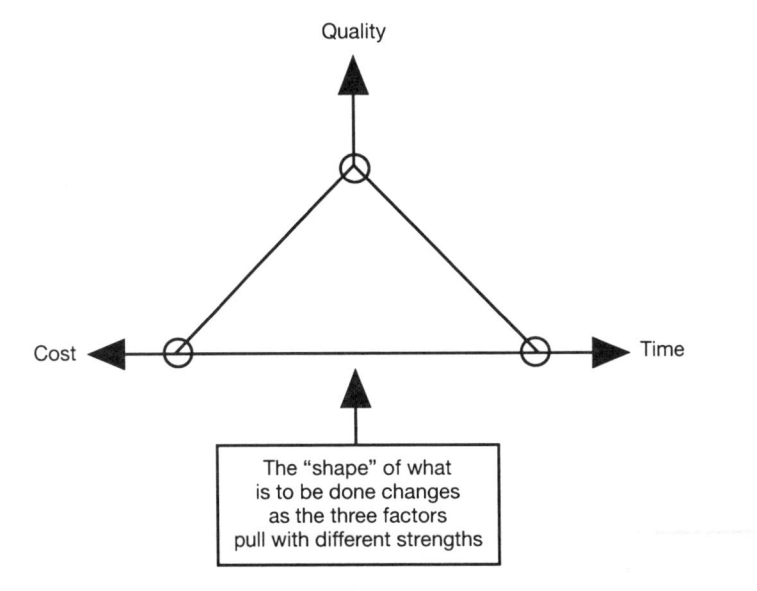

Fig. 2.8 The quality/time/cost balance

There is always a trade off here, and it is not always the easiest thing to achieve. Often a real compromise has to be made. Cost is often key in this. It would be easy to achieve the quality of output you want in many things, but only if cost were no object. And in most jobs budget considerations rank high. It is useful to get into the way of thinking about things in these terms, and doing so realistically so that you consider what is necessary as well as (or instead of?) what is simply desirable or ideal. In doing this there is one key factor that needs to be built in: a significant, and sometimes the largest, cost is your time. For some this is easy to cost. People like accountants or consultants will charge for their time by the day or hour and this makes them sensitive to just what costs are involved. In an organisation it is not just a question of dividing your salary to produce an hourly cost, you have to allow the many other costs of your being there. Factors will include everything from your office and office supplies to the cost of support – your secretary, for example, if you have one – and, of course, the cost of other benefits you receive in addition to salary.

It is worth your making this kind of calculation; the resultant figure may surprise you and it is a useful benchmark when considering many things in managing your time, whether you should make a journey, hold or attend a meeting and so on. Let me repeat, make sure by all means that what must be done to perfection is done in a way that achieves just that. Otherwise make sure you always keep in mind the balance to be struck between quality, cost and time; if you do not over engineer quality, seeking a standard that is not in some instances necessary or desirable, then you will surely save time.

Work smarter not longer

The answer to productivity in your job is not to work longer and longer hours. This may seem like a contradiction in terms. Surely if you put in more hours you will achieve more as a result? Yes, of course the direct answer to that is that you will. The point, however, is that there are limits. One thing we all have in common is the 24-hour day (unless of course there are creatures bending their tentacles to time management problems somewhere near Alpha Centuri). This is unchangeable and the amount of time we have to work with is finite.

It seems to be one of life's rules that jobs that are interesting do not allow a strictly 9–5 attitude; in part, this is probably why they are interesting, so I am not advocating this. After all, you get out of things what you put in and working hard must make a difference. But it is here that another balance must be struck for most people: that between work and home and outside interests and commitments. If you overdo the work, the other things – and they are important – suffer. What is more, damage, if damage is done, is insidious. You may not be aware of a difficulty until it is too late, and begins to cause some real problems.

The answer is to consciously seek to strike a balance, indeed you may want to lay down some rules for yourself about this, specifying maximum hours to work, travel or spend on specific things. In addition, for those readers who are managers, remember that the work capacity of the team you control is very much greater than yours, so it always makes sense to take a team view of things rather than just opting to do more yourself. Finally, excessively long hours worked can be misunderstood and make it appear to others that you are inefficient, which is presumably the reverse of how you want to appear. Long hours will be necessary on some occasions, to complete a particular project say, but in excess are likely to produce declining standards and run risks that make working smarter a much more attractive option. It is something to ponder (though not late into the night!) in order to make sure that you create a working pattern that is well balanced in this way.

Reward yourself

The final idea in this chapter is intended to motivate you towards better time management and to ensure you continue to think about it as you work. It has already been said that time management is not easy, that it demands a concerted effort, so you need to motivate yourself and give yourself some real reasons to make it work. You need something more than just getting to the bottom of your in-tray. In any case even the most effective person may never do this and, while what you achieve and how that is received is reward enough in some ways, what is wanted is something that is linked more specifically to your own success in managing your time.

It thus makes sense to set yourself specific time management goals and to link them to what that will do for you; to give yourself personal satisfaction so that you are very aware that succeeding in what you intend in time terms will make something else possible.

Such rewards may be seemingly small and personal (they do not have to make much sense to anyone else), but nevertheless an example may make the point. Take my work on this book. Having conceived and agreed the project, and this necessitates some time, the work falls into a number of stages: research and planning what the book will contain, structuring it (deciding the sections and sequence of points within each), actually writing it and final editing before the manuscript is sent to the publishers. Having discovered portable computers, I like to have some written work to do when I travel, and an overseas trip tends to contain quite a number of hours that can then be put to good use – on the flight and during otherwise wasted moments. Now the research and planning stage is difficult to do on the move as I need too many papers and too much space, so if I can complete that and have such a task at the writing stage as I leave on a trip then this gives me a manageable project to take with me. So, completing the initial work in time to fit in with a trip in this way becomes a private goal and the reward is that I have the right sort of task to accompany me on my travels. This may seem inconsequential but the point about it is that it is significant to *me*, and that is what matters.

If you can think in this kind of way and give yourself some sort of reward – better still a number of them – then your attention will be maintained on what time management can do for you. A major outcome of good time management is the ability to fit in projects that might otherwise be delayed, curtailed or omitted. Make such a pet project your reward, work out what is necessary in other areas to achieve it and you are just that much more likely to achieve what you want.

Everything reviewed in this chapter will help you create a better basis for becoming more efficient at time management. In particular it will help you to adopt the right attitudes in terms of the overall approach to your work, and in terms of specific areas of activity. Like so much that we approach with good intentions, thinking that an attitude makes sense is still a little way from implementing the principles and techniques it dictates. In real life, good intentions have a habit of deserting you at particular moments in favour of expediency – or panic! It may be easier to adopt a trigger to memory rather than a more all embracing intention. Saying that you will say 'no' to more requests may be difficult to apply consistently. However, some people find that resolving to count from one to ten before accepting unwelcome and avoidable requests without due consideration does work. Rather than being rushed into a 'yes', they are able to give a considered response which has the intention of avoiding the involvement. Of course, nothing like this is infallible. However, if such a ploy reduces this kind of acceptance in any sort of worthwhile way, then it is useful, and other areas may be susceptible to similar thinking.

All this will be made more effective if you and your work are essentially organised. In the next chapter we turn to the various ways of putting some order into the mess of reality.

3

Getting (and staying) organised

Creating the right time environment

'Despair is the price one pays for setting oneself an impossible aim'
GRAHAM GREENE

The Hitchhiker's Guide to the Galaxy had in large friendly letters on its cover, the words DON'T PANIC. Picking up this phraseology, it might be said that organisation is the friend of time management in the sense that being well organised is a major asset, perhaps a necessary preliminary, to being successful at working in a productive and effective manner. Poor organisation is insidious; everything takes just a little bit more time than it should and this adds up day by day, inevitably reducing effectiveness. This is true of even minor faults or omissions which, duplicated across a number of activities, can together have a significant effect and dilute efficiency.

At worst a lack of organisation causes real, even debilitating, problems. The poorly organised executive:

- cannot locate papers and information easily
- allow muddle to enter the diary, sometimes to the point of double booking
- is inclined to 'task hop', moving between tasks in an attempt to meet many and conflicting deadlines, completing things erratically
- is late and ill prepared for meetings
- allows paperwork to proliferate
- has no clear priorities
- works in a mess
- communicates poorly and keeps inadequate records

and, as a result, ends up duplicating effort, wasting time, missing deadlines, and delivering inadequate or insufficient results, even having apparently put in the time and effort required. Worse still in some ways, such poor performance is both visible to and affects others. Colleagues whose work overlaps with such a person are inconvenienced, the perpetrator collects a reputation for unreliability and not only is work affected but so are such things as personal promotion prospects.

Now all this is, I am sure, not painting a picture of *you* (the hopelessly disorganised will surely not even think to pick up a book on time management). But most of us will see a small part of ourselves in this kind of picture. You need little imagination to see how even some of the above can have very much the wrong kind of impact; and maybe, in some instances, memory confirms this view better than imagination!

It is all very well to stress the disadvantages of being disorganised, but, how do you get, and stay, organised? The key which was touched on in the last chapter, is having a plan. So we will return to that, looking not only at creating the plan but at working the plan. Beyond this there are numbers of different factors that contribute positively to a state of organisation. This chapter touches on an unashamed mixture of them. Some are simple ideas, though they can have a significant influence nevertheless. Others are more fundamental. All perhaps need some thought to fit them to your existing methods of going about your work, but many can also readily become habits so that you cease to use much time consciously thinking about their implementation. But first, back to planning.

Work the plan

There is more to this than just recording a list of 'things to do'. Tasks must be noted in the right kind of way and the way you review the list can usefully follow a pattern which, as a memory jogger, I have heard described as the LEAD system with the letters of the word 'lead' standing for:

- List the activities; this must be done comprehensively, though in note form as you do not want the list to become unmanageable
- Estimate how long each item will take, as a accurately as possible, and:

- **A**llow time for contingency as things always have a potential for taking longer than your best estimates (remember this is one of Murphy's famous laws); also allow time for regular tasks, the ongoing things that go on as a routine day by day
- **D**ecide priorities; this is key, and one of the most important aspects of time management for anyone (see Chapter 5)

Scan the plan, reviewing it overall probably once a day. (When I am in my office I like to do this at the end of each day, updating in the light of what has gone on during the day, followed by a quick review at the start of the day when the mail arrives. But what matters is what you find suits you.)

This process should become a routine. What other action may be necessary will depend on the pattern of your day and work. Something cropping up during the day may be either thought about and added to the list at the time or simply put on one side to be incorporated into the plan at the next review. One little thing I personally find useful is the ubiquitous yellow sticky paper pads (like 3M's *Post-it* notes) – whatever did we do before these things came along? – which can be used to make a brief note of something, appended to your planning sheet and then incorporated in more permanent form later.

This review, recording and review cycle is the heartland of time management. Proprietary systems set it out in particular ways, sectioning things and arranging them under headings; as has been said, if this helps that is fine, but many find their own simpler system works perfectly well. A sheet ruled into a number of spaces or the use of a second colour, or both, can make what may well be a full list easier to follow. If items are reliably listed and the list conscientiously reviewed then you will keep on top of things and certainly nothing should be forgotten.

The trouble with so many jobs (most?) is that the list of things to do is itself apt to get unmanageable – unless the tasks are batched.

Batch your tasks

Another overriding principle of good time management is to batch your tasks. Here again the proprietary systems all have their own methodology, and it is in some cases over complicated, certainly for my taste, but here again what works best for you is the only measure. What I am inclined to believe is more important than the precise configuration of the system here is the number of categories; three or four are ideal simply because that is manageable. It does not matter too much what you call them:

- PRIORITY
- IMPORTANT
- ACTION NOW
- OBTAIN MORE INFORMATION
- READING

are some of the options (and there are those who manage perfectly well with A, B and C). You will also need FILE (of which more in Chapter 6) and may consider other action categories such as TELEPHONE, DICTATE, WRITE, and DOCUMENT, and similar ones that are particular to your business and role in it such as PROPOSALS, QUOTATIONS or the names of products, departments or systems. Some of the implementation of this necessarily comes under the section on paperwork (see Chapter 6). The important thing at this stage is to work out how many and what titles of batches suit you and that this and the way you arrange your desk are not in conflict. A manageable number of batches of this sort can, if you wish, link physically to filing trays on your desk or some distinguishing mark on files themselves. (Incidentally, beware of colour coding as the basis for office-wide systems as a significant proportion of the world's population is colour blind.)

One grouping which can logically be commented on at this point is the events, most often appointments, which routine use of a diary can automatically batch together. Consider your diary next, then how you schedule appointments.

Use your diary effectively

Again there are matters here of personal preference, but a good clear diary system is a must. Many formal systems combine the conventional diary with their sophisticated version of the 'to do' list. I have commented on such systems elsewhere (see page 22). One thing that certainly works well, and which a loose-leaf system allows, is to have at one opening of a binder a convenient complete picture of your day, showing both appointments *and* things to do.

Confusion is caused in many offices over what constitutes the master diary. A desk diary often lives on the secretary's desk, another in the executive's pocket and sometimes there is more duplication such as with a wall planner. This needs to be clear, and usually necessitates regular updates between the executive and the secretary who must clearly both communicate and have an understanding about who does what.

Small things have an effect on efficiency. The diary should:

- show full details, certainly full enough to be clear. An entry that reads 'R.B. Lunch' tells you little – where is it, at what time is it, can you be contacted while you are out, how long will it last, and, not least, are you even going to remember in three weeks' time to whom R.B. refers? If you want a real horror story, I know of a case where all it said in someone's diary was the name of a town, with two days ruled out. He was away, presumably staying at a hotel, and had only told his family to contact him via his office. When one of his children was involved in an accident, it took two days before the message reached him. His diary was a copybook example of clarity thereafter.

- show how long is set aside for things (this will help a secretary decide what else can be fitted in).

- be completed in pencil so that alterations can be made without creating an illegible mess.

A planner element within a diary is very useful. Certainly I could not operate without one, and anyone who operates in a way that necessitates taking an overview of a period and seeing how things relate one to another is likely to find it invaluable. Perhaps the most important and useful difference between just an appointments diary and a time management system is if it is used to schedule *all* (or most) of the working time rather than just appointments. The two additions are tasks, actually setting aside time to work on a specific project, and thinking time so that planning and creative work is not carried out, as so often happens, only in gaps that are left between appointments and meetings. If this is done – leaving some space for the unexpected or reactive part of the work, whatever proportion that is – and linked to the concept of the rolling plan, you will stay much more organised and be able to judge much better how things are progressing, whether deadlines will be met and tasks completed.

Two final points: first, the diary is a vital tool, to be guarded and treated with respect. It is also therefore a good place to keep other key information, telephone numbers and other data you need at your fingertips, provided you do not overburden it so that it becomes too thick and unmanageable. Secondly, the computer is taking over some of these activities (and is referred to on page 95) and doing so very well for some, though the learning curve can be significant.

Schedule appointments with care

Appointments, transactions with other people, take up a major amount of many executives' time. Exactly when you programme them makes a real difference to your productivity. Allow sufficient time; one appointment running into another always causes problems. And always schedule a period of time, in other words a finishing time as well as a start time. It is impossible to do this with one hundred per cent accuracy, but it helps.

Think about:

- the potential for interruptions (an early meeting, before the office switchboard opens, may take less time because there are fewer interruptions)
- the location (where it is geographically makes a difference – see Chapter 8), and a meeting room may be better than your office, especially if you need to move what you are working on just before it starts.
- timing that makes it inevitable that it continues into lunch or a drink at the end of the day
- timing that restricts your ability to schedule other appointments, in the way that something mid-morning could mean there is not sufficient time to fit in another meeting before it, or after it and before lunch

And take especial care with gatherings that involve more than one person. You have to be accommodating here, but do not always consider others' convenience before your own – it is you that will suffer.

Record them clearly in the diary (see page 40) and consider separately the vexed question of meetings (see page 131).

While considering when to schedule appointments, it may be worth a slight digression to make a point about the most fundamental level of scheduling, that affected by your personal time clock. There is a serious, and useful, point to be made here. I will start with some personal comment.

Try as I might, I am not good at working late into the evening, though occasionally this is necessary for me as for others and I have to make the best of it. On the other hand, I am an early starter, I can get off to a good start on things comparatively early in the day. I think of myself as a 'morning person', know I will get more done in the first half of the day than in the second, and organise myself accordingly – something that affects what I schedule where in the day as much as my actual working practice and productivity.

There seems to be some scientific basis for this. We do all have rather different biological clocks and it seems to me to be unrealistic to ignore it. That is not to say that you can use this principle as an excuse – it is a short step from saying you are at your best in the morning to saying you cannot work effectively after a meal or when there is an 'R' in the month! But it is worth deciding what your own personal working pattern is and then working at both accommodating it and overcoming it. You may well not be able to work half a day, but you may be able to exercise some choice over when you do what, so that you can place different tasks in different parts of the day in order that those demanding your greatest concentration are tackled at a time when this is most likely . This is one of many areas where you will never achieve perfection, but that is no reason to ignore it; get things mostly right and you will be more productive and waste less time.

Clear your desk

There are those who are in no danger of causing a boost to the sales of furniture polish; their desks are totally covered with piles of paper and the wooden surfaces never see the light of day. These are the same people who, if asked about it, always reply, 'But I know where everything is'. They mean it too and some of them are right. But, and it is a big but, this kind of disorder rarely goes with good time management. It pays to be neat. It pays you and it may also pay the organisation for which you work. This is worth a slight digression. If you are employed by a large organisation you are not indispensable. Sorry, but it is true. What is more, it is incumbent in your responsibilities that you protect the continuity of operations and this includes thinking about what happens if you are, for any reason, not there. Even a short absence by someone on sick leave, say, can cause havoc. It takes others a while to locate things you were working on and, because of the difficulty, matters can be disrupted or delayed. Worse perhaps from your point of view, when you return and other people have been rifling through your system, you are not going to be able to find anything.

So resolve to keep your desk tidy. This means having a clear, and clearly labelled, system, one which is likely to be more specific than an 'In' and 'Out' tray and is reasonably intelligible to others. Having said all that, I recognise that there is a need in many people to have things visible, a belief that out of sight is out of mind and that this may lead to things being forgotten. This can be accommodated in part by your diary and planning system which can link to and identify where things are – in files or whatever – but still the need is there. Frankly I share it; there are certain kinds of thing I want visibly to hand and I am not as confident of having my fingers on everything unless that is so. One solution to this is to have a tray (or something bigger if necessary) that contains current project files. I have this to one side of my desk, and the top item in it is a list of those files that are there – because it is a changing population – which helps me check quickly if I am up to date with things. The list, which is in a transparent plastic folder, also records the status of projects and I find this very useful. Thus I believe it is possible to accommodate both views realistically; having key things to hand but keeping your desk clear. For most ordinary mortals it is a constant battle to keep things tidy, a battle that ebbs and flows, but one worth keeping a continuous eye on.

INTERMISSION
Take a break

Before moving to the next point, here is a useful thought that is logically separated from the main flow of the text by being set in a boxed section.

Time management is about . . . er, productivity . . . and er, . . . effectiveness. So . . . it . . . that is . . .

Sorry, I had to take a break for a moment there. I went to get a cup of tea (another cup of tea, if I am honest, and very nice too). This took maybe three or four minutes and I do not believe it extended the time taken to put the comments on this topic together, indeed the way they are presented was largely decided in some of that three or four minutes. After working on any intensive task for a while most people find their concentration flags, certainly mine does in writing. An occasional break is not a contradiction of the productivity you seek, it actually helps it. You return to your desk and your head is clearer; you feel refreshed and revived by stretching your limbs and can get back to the task in hand with renewed fervour.

This is particularly true of seemingly intractable tasks. Sometimes you can sit and puzzle about things for a long time and seem to get nowhere. After a break, as you start again, it suddenly seems clear – or at least clearer – and again time is saved as a result. Sometimes a break may be as simple as standing up and stretching, or making a cup of tea as I just did (but for me no job goes well without a regular supply of tea). Or it may be that you can benefit from something that takes a bit longer – you go to lunch even though you originally planned to do that an hour later, or you go for a walk. At one time I shared an office with someone who did this – the office was opposite a park and he had a particular circuit that took about ten minutes and was useful thinking time, perhaps being applied to something else apart from the job from which he had paused. This made a break yet was still productive. Alternatively, all you may need is simply to switch tasks for a moment, rather than stop work, in order to ring the changes.

In any event, a break is often much more productive than struggling on with a job when concentration is not adequate. Again it is something to utilise consciously and a pattern of such activity can become a useful habit if not taken to extremes.

Something to think about perhaps. Remember what Doug Kling is quoted as saying: 'Learn to pause . . . or nothing worthwhile will catch up with you'. Take a few minutes. It will test the idea. Me? I am going to have a bite of lunch before I even think about writing more; it will be more productive in the long run.

Avoid 'cherry picking'

Your approach to time management needs to be systematic. Some of the techniques that have been discussed here demand habit and a consistent approach. Some people are good at this, they make the plan, they list the priorities, they have a good diary and time system and are careful about their decisions and work practice in terms of how they affect the way they use time. But they then make one significant mistake which negates all this effort: they cherry pick.

That is they keep picking out jobs, possibly for one of the reasons that were reviewed earlier, such as because they like them. Whatever the reason, they keep rethinking their priorities and deciding that something else must be done first. They can spend so much time doing this that the plan never settles and time is not spent primarily on actioning it. Of course, a time plan is not static. It does need regular fine tuning, but this must not become an excuse for not sticking to it. If your plan is reviewed regularly and if the decisions made about it are good ones, then you can stick to it and will make more progress through the work list by doing so. Have confidence in your plan and resist being sidetracked by anything and it will work better for you.

Use abstracts

No one needs reminding of the amount of reading there is to do in most jobs. For some it is very important to keep up to date with the technical area their job involves, for others management processes themselves are worth regular study. In both cases the first task is to decide which, from the very many references published, should command your attention. This first selection exercise can be time consuming of itself before you actually study anything individually.

But here help is at hand. In most fields it is possible to subscribe to what are called abstract services. These are not expensive and from them you receive a regular list of what has been published on a given subject. Such a list does not just list the title of articles or papers (and books), but who wrote them, sometimes details of the author and, most important, a synopsis of the content. It is this latter point that lets you select with reasonable accuracy those items you judge you want to look at in more detail. You can then either turn up the source and read the item in full (scanning it first, no doubt) or, in some cases, the service will provide – for a small fee – a copy of a particular article without your having to purchase the full magazine or journal in which it appears.

If the thought of this facility appeals to you then you may want to check locally what services are available. Typically they will come from libraries, colleges, trade associations and professional bodies (management institutes may be able to help you), business schools and the like. If you find something that offers a service that appears to suit you then it is perhaps worth taking out a subscription for a short period and see whether it does save you time. If you find it does, and if it also helps you find information you might otherwise miss, it can then be economic to continue, in which case you have another continuing time saver on your side.

Highlight key facts

Amongst the mass of paperwork you have to read, file, keep or pass on there are some things contained in them that stand out. When you go back to a specific document you will likely have a key word, heading or section in mind and finding this can lead you straight to the key facts without combing through all the detail. But you need to be able to find the prompt element fast.

Highlighting things on paper is now easier than ever before because of the fluorescent highlighting pens in various colours produced by numbers of pen manufacturers. It is a small point perhaps, but one or more of these in your desk drawer is a great little time saver. They work well and any section, heading or word in a document marked with one really stands out, you cannot flick through a stack of papers and miss a page with a mark. They lead you to essentials, and I for one would not be without them. Like the yellow sticky sheets popularised by 3M, they are now a part of office life we cannot imagine not being there. If for some reason there is not one in your desk drawer, get some soon and give them a try. I predict you will quickly be hooked and become a regular user – fine, they are not expensive and they may save a few moments every day.

Insist on quality

There are fashions in management as in everything else. Management by Objectives enjoyed a vogue, Transactional Analysis (TA) became the way to look at communications, only to be replaced by something else. The issues, of course, remain but the focus turns to other things. Quality has always mattered, and always will, but is currently enjoying something of a special emphasis with Quality Management having been elevated into a major issue, often under the name Total Quality Management. This is no bad thing as anything that emphasises so important an aspect of corporate performance is all to the good.

Look at this for a moment on a more local scale. Consider your office, your department. Does it do a good job? Now you may well answer 'Of course', but how do you really know? Are there sufficient performance standards? Are you aiming specifically at achieving particular levels in all activities? For example, in the area of customer service, a bank may specify that no more than three customers should be in a single queue, that each should receive a greeting as they are attended to and that the customer's name should be used at the end of the transaction as they depart. Small points perhaps, but it is the summation of such points that add up to the standard of customer service that they intend to provide. Such standards are designed not simply to specify what should happen, but to make it more certain that the standards are achieved in practice.

You may have noticed (on your own time log?) how much time is sometimes spent sorting out things that have gone wrong. And this need not mean very wrong, but just falling short of the ideal by a small margin. Consider the bank example above again. If customers are kept waiting just a little too long some of them will comment on the fact, the cashier will apologise and perhaps explain, and the transaction will then proceed, usually without further problem. But it will take a little longer than it would otherwise, and with many hundreds of people seen each day at the counter this matters, not least to other customers whose wait is increased.

This is a simple example, but similar things will apply in your office. If you and your team get things right, and know what is necessary to get it right, then things will take less time, first because tasks will be efficiently performed, secondly because there will be less time wasted in any disruption caused by performance to a lesser standard.

Quality is a great friend of good time management. You should think about the standards of work with which you are involved, and clarify this area if necessary. Further, if there are moves within your organisation to embrace the likes of Total Quality Management, this will be worth supporting. There are set up costs and time needs to be invested also, but the equation is likely to work. Such initiatives will save time. *Do it right and the time it takes will be less* is a good general principle and can be applied to many areas of work. Quality saves time.

Decide on the nature of time: action or investment

Few people are bad time managers because they are idle. Certainly most of those with an interest in time management are busy people, but they are not getting everything done, or everything done thoroughly and on time. And the thing that gets neglected most is investment time, this is time taken now to ensure improvements or results in future – the planning and analysis and other such activities necessary to make progress in any area.

Categorising on your plan which category of time you are scheduling will help create a balance (it has already been mentioned that diary and 'to do' lists should schedule tasks – some evolve a code to differentiate between different sorts of task in this way). Thus the plan will show whether time is to be taken up with people (appointments, meetings etc.), with tasks (and whether they are action or investment orientated), and allow for the unexpected. And this will be able to be seen at a glance, maybe in the double opening of a loose-leaf book, so that fine tuning can take place if necessary. After all, time planning should be a guide and an assistance to the way you work, not a straitjacket that restricts you.

If you have a good feel for how much of your job should be spent in action time and how much in investment time, then you will be better able to maintain the balance you need, using the techniques of time management to create the working pattern *you* want. Time management is, and should be regarded as, a personal tool, something that you use your way to help you and not a standard approach that you must adopt in order to be efficient.

One panacea?

There is an old story told of a secretary to a much travelling and very senior executive. Asked by someone one day if he could see him, she replied that she was sorry but he was in Hong Kong. 'Abroad again' he replied, 'he's always overseas. Tell me, who does all his work while he's away?' She looked him straight in the eye and answered without hesitation: 'The same person who does it when he's here'. Some secretaries perhaps have such authority, but while the secretary is not a panacea, any more than the time management system sold on the basis that it will reorganise your life effortlessly is, they can help. Good secretaries cannot only be the recipient of some of your delegation, they can act as a regular prompt to good time management and take a genuinely active role in organising you, or your whole department.

The emphasis here is on *good* secretary, so the first job is to find the right one for you; and then, as we will see work *with* her to create the end result you want. So, what makes the right secretary?

The characteristics of the ideal secretary are legion. As well as typing, and sometimes shorthand, skills, she (it is usually she) must be familiar with an increasing array of office technology that typically stretches from coffee machine to computer. In addition, it helps if she is patient, is gifted with second sight and has two pairs of hands. But what of time management? Whether she has a natural or acquired organisational ability is difficult to assess at an interview, as is whether she really cares about such things. If you can do so, however, and only appoint a candidate who has characteristics of this sort then you will have a real asset on board in your battle to win the time war. Ask any questions you can think of that will give you information in this area, particularly about past experience in managing the diary and appointments of those she has worked for previously. This is also something to check in taking up references; this is always worth doing in almost any recruitment situation. At this level a phone call – with the permission of the candidate – to a last employer is probably the quickest check. It will be likely to give the best information anyway as people are reluctant to take the time or make the commitment to put references in writing.

There are two other important characteristics that you should seek. First, that she will work your way. This is important as there may be existing procedures and systems, as well as management style, that you need her to fit in with; on the other hand, always be ready to learn from her. There is no monopoly on good ideas, and in this area you should be on the look out for ideas from any source, the only criterion being that the ideas are useful. Secondly, that she has sufficient 'weight' or clout, that is she must be able to stand up for you with colleagues and others, to say 'no' on your behalf and to make requests on your behalf – and make it stick.

Achieve this and your attempts to control your time will have a permanent ally, one who will work with you to achieve what you want and who will, at best and with experience, take an active role in the process.

Communicate with your secretary

It is not a bit of good having a good secretary, one who is sympathetic to time management, and then not communicating with her. This is a classic example of something for which there is 'never time' but which, if you do find the time for it, will help you save much more time than this communication takes. Many executives start the day with a meeting with their secretary, perhaps when the mail arrives in the morning. You must decide what suits you best and also work out a way of keeping in touch and up to date with her if you spend much time out of the office, though modern communications make this easier than once was the case.

Your secretary must know how you work and know what you have on the go at any particular time. And she should if possible share your view of priorities, knowing what you are prepared to be interrupted for, which things and people rate most time and attention, and what must be actioned first. You need to review and organise the diary together, and over time it helps if you explain what you are doing and why so that she gets to know some of the detail beyond the letters and reports she types. Once she has some experience, more may well be possible. She can take the initiative on things, accompany you to certain meetings and ultimately run whole areas of your office life in a way that increases your utilisation of time dramatically. Find areas of real responsibility, let her look after them and make the decisions affecting them and it can pay dividends.

There is one prerequisite for all this and it is communication. It is no good coming back to the office after a trip and complaining that things have not been completed or that you now have a string of time wasting meetings in your diary, if lack of communication has caused this situation. So communicate clearly and regularly, and remember that includes listening.

As a footnote to this point it should perhaps be mentioned that working with a secretary necessitates that all the managerial techniques are brought to bear appropriately. This will include development, motivation and many more. A good relationship does not just happen, it demands some time up front – but the results can be very worthwhile.

Use a 'document parking' system

This point might equally have been listed under paperwork, but it is so useful a device that it deserves to come here. Perhaps the best explanation begins with the problem it solves. You may have many things on the go at any one time, and in physical terms they may consist of a single sheet of paper or a batch of correspondence. Many of them do not need action, or cannot be actioned immediately. This is what so often constitutes the ever present Pending Tray which makes many a desk groan under its weight. The net result is that you spend a great deal of time either shuffling through the heap to locate things, or checking things in there to see what you might in time do about them. The nature of some of the material makes the problem worse. Say one item can only be actioned when a certain monthly performance figure is published at the end of the month, then to keep checking it may well be both time consuming and useless as no action can be taken anyway. Further, constant reviewing can achieve little in advance of knowledge of the figures as the different possibilities in terms of what they might predicate are many.

If you suffer this sort of situation you need a parking place for such things, somewhere safe yet guaranteed to trigger prompt action at the appropriate moment. You need what is called a Prompt File (sometimes also called a Bring-Forward or, less elegantly, a Bring-up File). This means you take an item and decide when you will be able to progress it. This may be at a specific time (when the monthly figures arrive) or it may not (just six weeks on, or longer, at the start of the next financial year). Then you simply mark it with the date on which you next want to see it and file it, with other similar items, in date order. Then forget it. Waste no more time even thinking about it. You do not have to, because every day your secretary will check the file and bring anything marked with that day's date in to you with the morning mail. At which point you can either act or, occasionally, give it another date and move it forward.

A couple of provisos: first, you may want to limit the total quantity of items (or A–Z list them) as something will happen occasionally that means you need to take action earlier than you thought, and you will need to retrieve an item from the file and action it ahead of the date you originally set. Secondly, you may want to link it to a diary note, especially if you have no secretary. This is such a simple commonsense idea and everyone I know who runs one swears by it. If you do not already use this system, it takes very little time to set up. Why not give it a try?

Make use of checklists

How many times a week do you have to pause and think about how exactly to complete some routine task? Or you do it wrong or incompletely in respect of some detail? Even a tiny number of cases may make more checklists something that will save time, and save it both by preventing those pauses for thought and, more important, removing the necessity to do something again or the cost or inconvenience of not having it complete.

Consider an example: many companies have a form that is completed when a sales enquiry is received. Completing such a form does not only create a record and act as a prompt to further action, it can also act as a checklist, reminding you to:

- check the enquirer's job title as well as name
- ask how they heard of the company or product
- refer to an Account number
- check that you obtain any additional information such as credit details

plus as many more items as circumstances demand.

Many such routine tasks are not both routine and predictable, just as the conversation with the customer may take all sorts of routes and it is easy to forget those questions that might be considered optional, or at least of lesser importance. So a checklist helps. This can be either a form designed to be completed and acting in this way as the completion proceeds or a point of reference, literally just a note of what should be done. Some of these you may want to create for yourself and your department, others take the form of company 'standing instructions' and, despite being often categorised as 'yet another memo', may be well worth keeping.

All sorts of things lend themselves to this sort of approach. Fig. 3.1 gives one example, but there are many more, both long and short. You may like to make a mental note to look, in particular at things that provide assistance outside your own area of expertise. For instance, if you are a dunce with figures, do not throw into the bin that checklist concerning the procedure to reclaim expenses. It might just help you document them so that you can reclaim all the money you spent, or at least avoid the wrath of an accountant whose system is being ignored – and save you some time.

GETTING AND STAYING ORGANISED

ABSENCE REPORT

ABSENTEE'S SURNAME	INITIALS	MR: MRS: MISS: MS:	DATE

CLOCK NUMBER	PAYROLL NUMBER	SECTION/DEPARTMENT	SHIFT

ABSENCE STARTED ON   FINISHED ON

TOTAL No. OF DAYS SICK   (INCLUDING WEEKENDS & BANK HOLIDAYS)   TOTAL No. OF WORK DAYS

REASONS FOR ABSENCE: PLEASE ✓

- ○ HOLIDAY (PAID)
- ○ HOLIDAY (UNPAID)
- ○ SICKNESS IN FAMILY
- ○ DEATH IN FAMILY
- ○ PERSONAL SICKNESS
- ○ ACCIDENT ON DUTY
- ○ ACCIDENT OFF DUTY
- ○ SUSPENSION
- ○ INDUSTRIAL ACTION
- ○ NO REASON GIVEN
- ○ UNION DUTY
- ○ JURY SERVICE
- ○ EXCUSED ABSENCE
- ○ UNEXCUSED ABSENCE
- ○ REASON GIVEN IN COMMENTS SECTION

HAS DOCTOR'S CERTIFICATE BEEN PROVIDED?	○ YES	○ NO
HAS STATUTORY SICK PAY BEEN CLAIMED	○ YES	○ NO

DOCTOR'S NAME   HOSPITAL
TEL. No.   TEL. No.

COMMENTS

DECLARATION BY EMPLOYEE

I UNDERSTAND THAT KNOWINGLY MAKING A FALSE DECLARATION OF MY REASON FOR ABSENCE AND CLAIMING PAYMENT FOR SUCH ABSENCE RENDERS ME LIABLE TO INSTANT DISMISSAL. I UNDERSTAND THAT TO UNDERTAKE ANY OTHER EMPLOYMENT WHILST CLAIMING PAYMENT FOR ABSENCE RENDERS ME LIABLE TO INSTANT DISMISSAL.

I CLAIM THE PAYMENTS TO WHICH I AM ENTITLED UNDER THE RULES OF STATUTORY SICK PAY AND THE COMPANY STATUTORY PAYMENT SCHEME WHICH EVER APPLIES. I AUTHORISE THE DEDUCTION FROM MY PAY AND SICK PAY ANY SSP OR STATE BENEFITS SPECIFIED FOR DEDUCTION IN MY TERMS AND CONDITIONS OF EMPLOYMENT AND SICKNESS PAYMENT SCHEME RULES.

I DECLARE THAT THE INFORMATION GIVEN ABOVE IS TRUE AND CORRECT

SIGNATURE   DATE

NAME OF: SUPERVISOR/FOREMAN/MANAGER   DEPARTMENT
DID ABSENTEE REPORT ABSENCE?   ○ YES   ○ NO
                                            TIME: _____
REPORTED TO: BY: DATE: _____

OFFICE USE ONLY
- ○ SALARY PAYMENT TO BE MADE.   ○ WILL MAKE UP TIME
- ○ DEDUCT FROM SALARY .... DAYS PAYMENT.

WHITE COPY: TO PERSONNEL DEPARTMENT. PINK: TO WAGES DEPARTMENT. YELLOW: RETAIN IN BOOK

Fig. 3.1 *Drake Office Systems Ltd **Example of 'checklist' style forms**

This kind of documentation is clearly not only useful to record information, but the items listed act as a prompt to remind you of necessary action. Such forms (this one is from a range designed and produced by Drake* and available in carbonated sets) can be purchased as standard items (there are many different ones available so this may be a useful area to check) or home produced to do just what you want.

Be realistic

Your time log exercise will give you a clear idea of the pattern of your day. It will show how much time you spend, on average, on different things and what the worst problems are of keeping on schedule. Once you start to really plan, to estimate how long things are going to take, and write down an intention as to how your day should go, you will quickly find that the difficulties do not evaporate. Planning is a basis from which to seek improvements to your time utilisation and you must be realistic about it and seek to design a methodology which truly fits your job and way of working. That is not to say you should preserve the bad habits, and if you think about this area seriously you will find you have some; everybody does. But you need to reflect on the reality of what must be done.

If you spend a great deal of time on the telephone, or in meetings (necessary ones), or have to do things at particular times of day to fit in with other people or to allow contacts across an international time zone, then so be it. These things must be accommodated. You can reduce the waste of time and control to some extent the interruptions, but you will still find that perhaps only a proportion of your time is concerned with doing clearly planned things. This may be 50 per cent or 60 per cent on average – but averages here are not very meaningful; what matters is the productivity of your time. If your day is only 30 per cent plannable, or 80 per cent, then that may be quite normal. What matters is to plan the controllable aspects and control the random elements that affect the rest of your time, accepting that there will be interruptions, including some productive ones, that there are necessary reactive elements to what you do, that you need some social interaction with others in your workplace and that all this – the routine and creative – has to be accommodated. To try to plan away from

* Drake Office Systems Ltd

the realities which must be accommodated will only succeed in wasting time, though to interpret unnecessary things as realities will do the same.

Research shows that starting from a situation where you have not really considered any formal time management, a conscientious review and effort to improve your situation can provide an improvement of 10–20 per cent of your time utilisation. This is true almost regardless of the particular pattern of your work, and it is very significant and worth aiming for – at best you can add as much as a day each week to your effective time! So do not struggle with the impossible, some things in your job must be the way they are, but look realistically at what can be done, work at it, and you can achieve real, lasting and very worthwhile changes to your performance.

All the techniques mentioned in this chapter, and more no doubt, can help you become more time efficient. To show that any positive effect is not entirely at random, we will turn to the thought of giving time management some focus.

Directing the techniques at particular result areas

Everything you do in time management terms is designed to effect efficiency, effectiveness and productivity; to enable you to do more and to do everything better than would otherwise be the case, so as to achieve the results your job demands. But there are advantages to be gained en route to these ends, and these are useful in their own right. Bearing them in mind can help you adopt some of the methodology necessary to an organised way of working and make the whole process easier. Such advantages include:

- having a clear plan, knowing and having an overview of what must be done – the first step to successfully completing the tasks on your list. Such clarity will make adequate preparation more likely and this can reflect directly on achievement)
- having a clear link between things to do and overall objectives which is a sound recipe to keeping on track
- being better organised (e.g. not wasting time looking for things)

- your memory coping better with what you actually need to remember (the systems take care of some of this for you, and it is not necessary to keep everything in your head)
- being better able to identify and concentrate on the essentials
- wasting less energy on irrelevancies
- making better decisions about how things should be done (and better business decisions generally)
- better coordination of tasks (progressing certain things in parallel saves time)
- having a greater ability to cope with or remove distractions and interruptions
- cultivating the habit of greater self discipline about time matters, which makes consistency of action progressively easier
- a greater ability to cope with the unexpected and emergency elements of any job

Any of these are useful, but some may be more useful to you than others, at least at a particular moment or stage. It may be useful to look for the particular advantage you want, wasting less energy on irrelevancies or, more specifically, attending fewer meetings, for example. Or you may wish to adopt methods that will have precisely the impact you want. This is not to say that all those listed above do not have a good general effect on productivity. They do. But they produce additional, and more personal advantage also. You will achieve more, and get greater satisfaction from the results you achieve. In addition, you may have more time to develop what you do and how you do it, and motivate yourself and your staff, all of which can potentially improve things still further. And it may remove some of the things that create the feeling that a job is 'hard work' (which is different from 'working hard'). In my experience the latter nearly always a prerequisite of success. You do not want tasks to constantly put you in mind of trying to nail jam to the wall when a little organisation will ensure they go smoothly. Or at least not *too* many!

This list of advantages makes both a suitable summary to this section and preliminary to all that follows. If you bear these and other advantages in mind they can help you implement specific changes with clear ends in mind.

So far we have taken a view of the job to be done somewhat in isolation, as if work somehow managed to proceed smoothly away from what I referred to earlier as the mess of reality – the people, the meetings, the paper, the interruptions and . . . but you know only too well the scenario you face day to day. In the next chapter we turn to matters that so often seem to act to dilute the best intentions of all who strive to be good time managers: that is interruptions and time wasters.

4

Controlling the time wasters

The inherent difficulties and how to deal with them

'The art of being wise is the art of knowing what to overlook'
WILLIAM JAMES

Nothing is more annoying than . . .

There is not anything half as distracting . . .

Nothing is more annoying than being interrupted except being interrupted unnecessarily – more than once. And, as you may have noticed, it just happened to me – twice. Interruptions can take many forms. People are behind many of them, in person at your elbow, on the telephone or shouting from afar. Also involved are emergencies, fire drills, computer malfunctions, visits to the stationery cupboard, accepting deliveries (even just of a fax), lunch, coffee and what – for the sake of delicacy – might be called comfort breaks; all take up time, usually more than they reasonably should.

In the last chapter clear and positive planning was advocated and yet (this was touched on) however sensible that sounds, however much you want to set a plan and follow it, things seem to conspire to make it impossible. I seem to recall reading a survey somewhere that said that the average time a manager spent working uninterrupted was less than 15 minutes. Many will endorse that all too easily. Interruptions and other time wasting intrusions are endemic. You either collapse under the weight of them, becoming fatalistic and believing that they are inevitable and there is nothing that can be done to reduce them. Or you go on the offensive. This may well be the most obvious example of the need not to let perfection be the enemy of the good, because you will always get some interruptions. But you *can* reduce their number; and, if you want to be effective at time management and reap the rewards, you must do so.

If you worked in a hermetically sealed room safe and protected from the outside world, if you had no interactions with people and the telephone never rang, you would no doubt get a great deal more work done. But it would be a sterile environment and you would in many ways be less creative and less effective, because what you do in business draws strength from the various interactions and stimulæ around you. And in any case the sterile environment is simply not one of the options. So, the intention here is not to cut yourself off from the outside world completely, nor to avoid legitimate interruptions some of which can be positive, but to minimise the real time wasters and replace some of them with more time effective ways of achieving what we want.

We start by looking at three important aspects of one of the greatest timewasters, certainly the greatest procrastinator: yourself. This is an area of habit and of some natural human characteristics that need fighting, and I think fighting is the right word, for there are things here that we tend to return to again and again with time being frittered away on every occasion we do so. Putting off the difficult is one of the worst instances of this.

Do not put off the things you find difficult

The time wasted here can occur in two ways. First, decision making is delayed, then implementation is delayed and both let time leak away. Let us take a dramatic example to put something clearly difficult in mind. Imagine you manage a group of people, one of whom is performing badly. Action must be taken, and there are only ever three options here: put up with it (which is not to be recommended), develop or persuade the person to perform more effectively, or dismiss the poor performer.

The reasons for the poor performance may need checking, which can be difficult, so the temptation is to put it off – and time goes by. Or you decide that development of some sort is necessary and, if it is something you have to do, this is delayed – and time goes by. Or perhaps you decide it is a hopeless case and dismissal is the only solution. But no one really enjoys firing someone. It is difficult so you put it off, perhaps to try and think of the best way of doing it (there is *no* painless way). And throughout the entire process the thought keeps coming to mind that 'maybe it will get better'. This kind of thinking can be all too common and you can probably equate it with many difficult tasks you have had to tackle.

Now it seems to be a sad fact of life that difficult things do not get easier if they are left for a while. Worse, in many cases what starts out as a bit difficult rapidly becomes very difficult if left and often breeds additional problems along the way. Think again of the scenario mentioned above. What are the costs of continuing poor performance if things are allowed to run? And what is the nature of them? In other words, how else will things become affected? For example, if the poor performer was a salesman the cost can be measured in the revenue of lost sales, but, depending on the nature of the poor performance, may also be counted in terms of lost customer goodwill which might be even more costly in the long term.

So do not put off the things, whatever they may be, large or small, that you find difficult. Of course, the thought, consideration, checking, or whatever needs to be done, must be done and in many contexts should not be skimped, but once you are able to make the decision or take the action, or both, then there is merit in doing so. Watch out for any tendency you have in this respect, controlling it can save considerable time and aggravation.

Do not put off the things you do not like

There is a difference between what you find difficult and what you simply do not like. The likely effect of delay and avoidance of tasks is very similar here to that referred to above, and I will not repeat a similar example here, but the motivation is different, though none the less powerful.

There may be numbers of reasons for disliking doing something: it involves something else you do not like (and that for the best motives, perhaps doing something necessitates a visit to a regional office, something that will take up a whole day and involves an awkward journey), or, more often, the dislike is minor – it is just a chore. This is perhaps the chief reason why administration is so often in arrears. It is boring and there are other things to do and . . . but you doubtless know the feeling.

The only real help here is self discipline and a conscious effort in planning what you do to make sure that such things do not get left out and that this, in turn, does not lead to worse problems. Some flagging system to highlight things on your list may act as a psychological prompt. Experiment here to see if it makes a difference.

If all this seems minor and you disbelieve the impact of this area, it is likely that any time log exercise you undertake will confirm the danger. Again it seems simple, but the correct approach can save a worthwhile amount of time.

Beware of your favourite tasks

This is potentially even more time wasting that putting off things that you do not like or you find difficult, and often the most difficult to accept. But many people spend a disproportionate amount of time on the things they like doing best and, perhaps also, do best. This is perfectly natural and there are a variety of reasons for it. An important one is that any concentration on what you like is what seems to produce the most job satisfaction. This is fine if that satisfaction comes simply from doing whatever it is and the thing itself is necessary, but the danger is that you may be prone to over engineering as it is called, doing more than is necessary, putting in more time and sometimes producing a standard of quality or excellence that is just not really necessary.

But there can be more sinister reasons for this practice, for example, it may be because you:

- are using one task to provide an excuse to delay or avoid others (the difficult things, perhaps), telling yourself, with seeming reason, that you are too busy to get to them
- are concerned about delegating (a subject to which we return) and worry that a task is not a candidate for this, so you go on doing it yourself and go on over engineering
- find the work conditions of one thing too tempting, such as a low priority job that involves visiting an attractive city new to you, for

instance; this is something that is compounded by the opposite being true of the priority task

- find some aspect of possible over engineering fun; as an example, this happens to some people who have a fascination with computers, and they spend hours devising, say, a graphic representation of some figures when something simpler would meet the case just as well
- do not know how to go about something else and use the familiar as an excuse for delay or inappropriate delegation.

All these and more can cause problems in this way. It is frankly all too easy to do, we are all prone to it, probably all do it to some extent and thus all have to be constantly on our guard against it. Usually it continues because it is easy not to be consciously aware that it is happening. The answer is to really look, and look honestly, as you review your tasks and your regular work plan for examples of this happening. Better still look for examples of where it might happen and make sure that it does not. Of all the points in this book, I would rate this as in the top few best potential time savers for most people. Do not be blind to it – it is so easy to say, 'But *I* don't do that'. Check it out and see how much time you save. And, who knows, maybe some of the extra things you can then fit in will become tomorrow's favourite tasks.

Self-generated interruptions can be surprisingly time consuming and are one of the surprises that often emerge from a personal time log. It is easy to be blind to them and, at the risk of being repetitive, it is logical to watch for these before the ones involving other people. Not that they are insignificant. The reverse is true, and we turn now to how to bring some control to bear on them.

Handling personal interruptions

Business would be nothing without people. This is a pity in some ways as you would otherwise certainly have a great deal more time. You cannot remove the people, but you can make attempts to control their unscheduled disruption of your work. Consider the effect first. Imagine someone sticks their head into your office and says, in those immortal words: 'Do you have a minute?' You may not know what it is about, but of one thing you can usually be absolutely certain: it will not take only a minute! Interruptions may take any amount of time;

you could find half the day disappearing on an unscheduled meeting. Now continue to imagine, let us say, that the visiting someone interrupts and takes up 15 minutes of your time. How long does that interruption last? Not 15 minutes, but just a little more as you have to get yourself back into whatever work was interrupted and this may take a little time, and possibly still more time to get up to the peak of performance that you were working at previously. This effect is worth bearing in mind or you can be apt to underestimate the impact of interruptions. Fig. 4.1 makes this clear, showing how a number of interruptions during a period reduce performance of a task to nothing for some time and how that performance takes a moment to pick up and then may not reach the same peak. Time logs often show a significant loss of time in this way, as much as 25 per cent of total working time sometimes being affected.

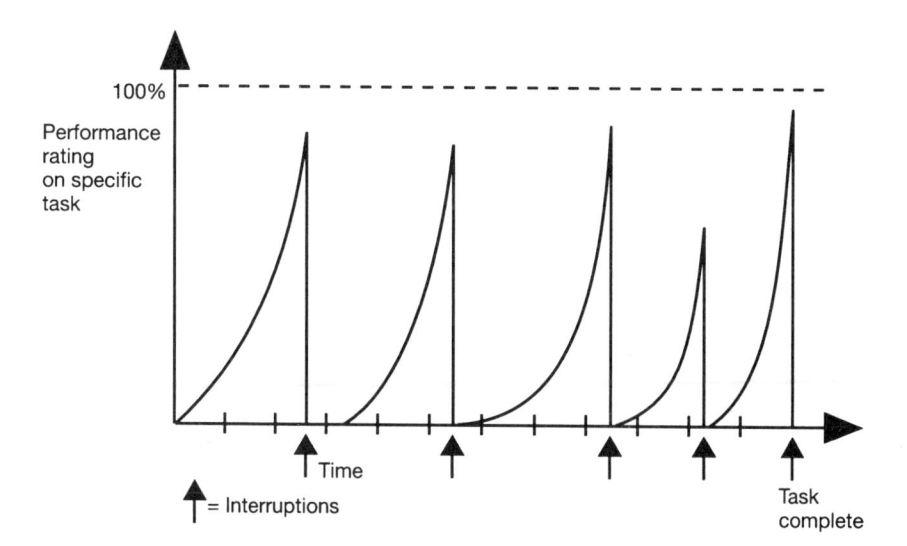

Fig. 4.1 The effect of interruptions on performance

Of course, some interruptions are in themselves useful. You want to have the discussions they consist of, but not at that moment; on the other hand some are a complete waste of time. So how do you minimise them?

There are essentially four responses:

(i) *Refuse them:* simple; you just say 'No' and send the person away. Sometimes it is that easy, it was not an important matter, it can be sorted without your help and does not crop up again. Alternatively the person will recontact you at another time. Of course it is more difficult if it is your boss rather than a colleague, but you can acquire a mutual respect for each other's time in a working relationship (more of this in Chapter 7). Then again, sometimes this route is simply not possible, whatever it is is simply too important and should take precedence, as with an unscheduled customer visit perhaps.

(ii) *Postpone it:* say you cannot pause right now, but offer to fix a time for a discussion — or better still suggest one convenient to you — this still appears helpful and means you can choose when to hold the required discussion. What is more, it is a technique that will make some interruptions go away with the response that it 'doesn't really matter'. Try this, you might be surprised how many never return.

(iii) *Minimise them:* here you agree to pause, but you put a time limit on it — 'I can let you have ten minutes'. If you do this, *always* stick to the time. In fact, by being disciplined in this way, you can create a reputation about your attitude to time and command respect, and this too will reduce interruptions a little.

(iv) *Prevent it:* in this case you need to instigate a system which provides some time guaranteed free of interruptions. You can plan and work this with a secretary, booking time for a job and treating it like an important meeting. But it can be simpler than that, and I know of cases where, even in an open plan office, people have agreed to respect a sign saying 'DO NOT DISTURB'. There is one proviso here: do not overuse this system. If you are never available you will still finally get interruptions or things you want to hear about will pass you by and something may go wrong as a result.

There is one other possibility that is available to some: you can *miss interruptions* by being somewhere else. You may have the kind of job where you can choose where you work. Spending the first two hours of the day finishing that report at home before you come into the office may be a good option if you are able to do it. Over the years I have met people who tell me they have found a variety of strange places to repair to for a while to get the peace and quiet that improves productivity so much on some kinds of task. These have included one person who visited the Public Library Reading Room which was conveniently a minute or two's walk from his office, a nearby park (not with papers on a windy day), and, for those who travel on business and sometimes have to stay in hotels, actually planning to take work along and stay on till checkout time rather than leaving first thing in the morning. Two days of my work on this book was carried out in an hotel in Malaysia (when a training course was postponed). The only interruption during the entire time was the next cold drink arriving, but it was only possible because I never travel without having some work with me for such occasions – a good habit, I think, and somehow appropriate that it should occur with work on a book of this particular title!

Some ideas to reduce the number of drop-in visitors appear in the boxed paragraph overleaf.

ACTION TO REDUCE THE NUMBER OF DROP-IN VISITORS

Some you want to see, some you do not, and many can be a complete waste of time. So, unless they are really useful or important (or a prime link in the grapevine) try some of the following to put them off:

- insist on appointments whenever necessary
- establish, and publish, 'do not disturb' times
- acknowledge them, but arrange another time to see them
- remember it is easier not to start some discussions than to get out of them quickly (especially ones starting: 'I wonder if you could help?'. Possibly, but should you? Or is there another way or time to help?)
- brief your secretary and other staff both to cope with more and to be firm where necessary
- use effective communications to reduce queries
- decide and inform regarding what needs to be originated in writing (though inappropriate memo writing can also be time wasting)

and for the really awkward/difficult:

- do not invite them to sit down
- set a time limit
- indicate an ending being soon ('One more thing, then I must get on . . .')
- initiate other action to make any drop-in unnecessary, including visiting them

and, above all:

- say 'no', or even 'NO' more often; you can be firm without being (too) rude.

Handling telephone interruptions

Sometimes you want to be immediately accessible, on other occasions you can get a secretary to act as a buffer taking calls in the first instance and checking who is calling. Clear briefing can rapidly establish those you will pause for, those to arrange for you to call back and those to forget.

If you take the call yourself you are at a considerable advantage compared with facing the head round your office door: the caller cannot see you, and there are many who do not regard saying they are busy, in a meeting, just leaving the office or similar statements as too much of a white lie. I even know someone who plays the noise of voices on a dictating machine to give callers the impression that a meeting really is going on! Just like physical interruptions, you can aim to avoid, postpone or minimise them, and additionally you may wish to devise special responses to particular kinds of call.

For example, how many calls do you get from sales people in a week? Enough for it to be a distraction most would say. Some of them are useful, some you already do business with and want to maintain the contact. But others you need to get rid of quickly. Most of us are reasonably polite, and we do not like to be rude to people, but consider: only one minute spent on the telephone just to be polite, assuming you spend this with only three telesales people every week, is two and a half hours in a year. And to save this time you still do not need to be rude. Find out at once what they are selling – then you can listen if you want – otherwise a neat sentence really early on will get rid of them fast: 'I am sorry, that would not be of interest and I am afraid I am too busy to speak now. Goodbye'. Then put the phone down. You can always suggest another time to call back if you think a word with them would be useful.

People know and understand, from their own experience, that the phone can be intrusive and tend to be more understanding of your not necessarily welcoming a call at a particular moment. You can use this and save time.

All matters of handling these kinds of people interruption require the normal people handling skills: tact, diplomacy, but also suitable assertiveness. These need to be deployed in the right mix and to the appropriate degree. If you are seen as insensitive and assertive to the point of rudeness this may well be destructive of relationships. But if you effectively lie down and ask to be walked on, then it should be no surprise when you are treated like a doormat.

The boxed paragraph adds some suggestions for reducing call intrusion.

> ## ACTION TO REDUCE TELEPHONE INTERRUPTIONS
>
> All sorts of calls can be problematical, some just because they interrupt, others because you do not want (or should not have to) deal with them anyway, still more because they last unnecessarily long or the person at the other end is a chatterbox. Some of the following may help with some of the calls you wish to discourage, or prompt further ideas:
>
> - check the information on which the switchboard operator assigns calls, and rebrief if necessary
>
> - brief your secretary well if you have one
>
> - ask a colleague to take calls for a period (you might swap time doing this)
>
> - create clear 'do not disturb' times
>
> - use an answer phone system (though watch the negative side of this, for example the image presented to outsiders, especially customers)
>
> - specify to others when to call you ('Why not call me back between two and three?' 'Please ring before ten, I will be tied up later in the morning') whenever possible
>
> - remember delegation will direct calls to others on particular topics they will in future deal with for you
>
> - give people the names of your secretary, assistant or others (many people who if told you are busy will simply call back, even if asked if someone else can help; if you actually say: 'If I am not here then do talk to Mary, my secretary, I will make sure she knows about it' or similar, their reluctance to talk to someone else declines)
>
> - be aware of the time wasting nature of social chatter and aim to curtail it before it gets out of hand (do much, waste so much time; none, and the world would be a less interesting place)
>
> - set a time limit ('OK, tell me about it now, but will you keep it to ten minutes as I have a visitor due soon' – people would much rather know than be cut off half way through, so this need not seem rude)
>
> - indicate the end is near, by using words like 'finally', 'before I ring off' to make it clear to a caller you, at least, intend to stop soon
>
> - failing all else, be rude; or at least consider whether part of the problem may be that you are just too concerned to be polite (fitting in time when the phone rings can become a reflex; we say 'sure . . . 'rather as we answer 'fine' when asked how we are, however we actually feel)

Even more important is the resolve and tenacity which you put into establishing approaches here. Some people are conspicuously more successful than others at avoiding interruptions; if so they doubtless work at it. Precedents are easily set, for good or ill. There is a great deal to be gained by getting things right in this area and that includes ensuring you are seen in the right kind of way.

That said, are there any other kinds of interruption and can these too be minimised? Bearing in mind (again) the cumulative impact of time savings, a couple of examples follow to conclude this chapter.

Save time getting through to people on the telephone

I can never quite come to terms with this one, it always seems unbelievable how much time is wasted dialling, redialling and holding on the telephone, much of it these days listening to a unique and repetitive form of music which has been known to send even the most sane into unreasonable states. The simplest way of avoiding all this is to get your secretary to obtain calls for you, but her time is valuable too so this is not the complete answer.

What does make a real difference is a modern telephone. This is a form of new technology I really warm to. They are not so complicated that they put you off and there are specific features that are real time-savers. For example:

- if you have the ability to store all the common numbers you use this will save you having to dial them, a couple of digits and the phone does the rest
- many will also redial (for example, if the chosen number is busy first time) and some will go on and on dialling automatically until they get through
- a loudspeaker means that if you have to hold on (listening to the music) then your hands are free and work can continue

The same kind of features may affect your sending of faxes, if you use a personal office machine. From personal experience I have observed a marked saving in time from the machine I have used day to day now for the last couple of years which has similar features. This is another, perhaps seemingly small, point which can make such a difference to your time. And each time you discover one the time saving adds up just a little more.

Make messages accurate

Without a doubt a vast amount of time must be wasted in offices around the world because of inaccurate or incomplete messages. Time is wasted wondering what things are about, with things said once being repeated and things having to be repeated or repaired because of errors or breakdowns in communication. There are bound to be times when you are away from the office, and even if such absences are brief or infrequent, a good message system in your office will save you time and prevent possible misunderstandings which can have other effects.

You need a message form that is designed for you. The information you want may not be exactly that on the forms that commercial stationery companies sell. In this way it acts as a checklist for those around the office as to the information you want noted. Small differences here are important. For example, a section for ACTION TAKEN as well as ACTION REQUIRED tells you exactly how far a conversation proceeded and allows follow up without repetition. Fig. 4.2 shows an example, but do not copy it, adapt it.

I believe such forms should be in a style that declares their importance – after all one lost message may change history (or at least cause major corporate or personal inconvenience). You must decide what suits. Maybe a full size page is best (it means it can clip together with other papers to make a neat file as well as being more visible); maybe it should be on coloured paper so that it stands out amongst other office paperwork.

All this helps; so too does clear briefing as to what should be dealt with, passed on, how quickly and in what circumstances. For example, do you want everything sent on to a conference you attend for a couple of days, or only certain things? What about people – who is told where you are and who not? And so on. It is a waste of everyone's time if you get even accurate message, if you are simply going to pass them back to the office or leave them till your return. I remember wondering about such things at a course I ran for an hotel group. One of the

TELEPHONE MESSAGE

For: **Name:** _____ **Date:** _____

Department: _____ **Time** _____

From:

Name:	Job title:
Company:	
Address:	
Tel:	Fax:

MESSAGE: _____
_____
_____
_____
_____

ACTION TAKEN: _____ ACTION PROMISED: _____
_____ _____
_____ _____
_____ _____

Message taken by:	Copies to:

Fig. 4.2 Example of message form

managers attending got a message during one of the lunch breaks and came back to the table looking a bit down. Someone asked him what the message was, and he explained that a guest had committed suicide in his hotel. Not knowing exactly what this would mean, I asked him about it and it transpired that a procedure existed to inform the police and do everything else necessary. In this case it had all been done and there was no action for him to take. So I asked why his assistant had called him. He looked rather confused and admitted he did not know. I suppose they thought he ought to know, but why put this on his mind during a course, especially as there was no action to be taken? Certainly, if it had been me, I would rather not have known until I got back to base.

So decide what you want to know, how messages should be taken and when, where and how they should be passed on. It is one more small thing that adds a little more to good time utilisation.

Although the areas of potential time saving are mounting up as this review progresses, and that is in itself useful, it must always be kept in mind why the time is needed. To do the tasks the job demands is too simplistic a way of putting this as, in most if not all jobs, some things are more important than others. In the next chapter we turn specifically to priorities, the first things first principle from which this book takes its title.

5

First things first
Setting and sticking to priorities

'The secret of success is consistency of purpose'
BENJAMIN DISRAELI

It may be a little late to be stating absolute fundamentals, but there is one fact upon acceptance of which much, if not all, of an individual's approach to time management must be based. This is simply that none of us can do more than one thing at a time. No one – ever. It is no use quibbling. Yes, of course there may be some overlap, but that is not the same thing at all. Like the 24-hour day, we are all stuck with this fact, and the fact is that what we do (and do not do, or spend less time on) is ultimately a crucial measure of success.

Time management is certainly about using methods that will increase the amount of real effective time available to you, but it is also about ordering the work within that time to produce a focus on the right things. As such it is about priorities as much as it is about anything else. This section addresses a number of issues under this heading, and aims to give you some ideas to help. Long term, however, one of the things that really separates the time efficient from others is their ability to decide on their priorities easily and accurately. That is not something anyone gets one hundred per cent correct, and is perhaps something that only comes with experience, but it is worth working towards.

We start by going back in time to consider a principle which has considerable application in the present day.

Pareto's Law

Before you can work effectively in deciding priorities, you have to come to grips with their importance. This sounds obvious no doubt, and of course you may say some things are obviously more important than others. But it is very easy to underestimate just how much this concept influences what you need to do, indeed just how much it influences your inherent effectiveness. The Italian economist, Vilfredo Pareto, many years ago recognised the truism that carries his name (he showed that 20 per cent of the population owned 80 per cent of the national wealth) and which is now more commonly called the 80/20 rule. It links cause and effect in a ratio and, although this is not represented absolutely accurately in real life, an approximately 80/20 ratio is found in many business activities, sometimes with a precision that is considerable. This means that for instance:

- 20 per cent of a company's customers are likely to produce 80 per cent of its revenue
- 20 per cent of factory errors are likely to cause 80 per cent of quality rejects

and it applies specifically in terms of the issues reviewed here also:

- 20 per cent of meeting time results in about 80 per cent of decisions made
- 20 per cent of items to read that pass across your desk produce 80 per cent of the information you need in your work

and, most important of all, *20 per cent of your work time probably contributes around 80 per cent of what is necessary to success in your job.* So, it is enormously important to reflect this in the way you operate so that attention is focused on those key issues that have this dramatic effect.

You may not be able to readily identify exactly which of your tasks have this effect. Some things will be clear, others you may need to think about. Have a look at your job description, at your time log too and make yourself think through and decide just what it is about what you do that has the greatest effect. It may not always be obvious for all sorts of reasons. You may take some key things for granted; for instance, forgetting once they have become a routine how important they are. Certainly you are unlikely to find a direct relationship between such a list of key issues, if you compile it, and the things your time log shows you spending the most time upon. Just this simple review may prompt you to make some changes to your work pattern. Clear objectives and a clear job specification, together with a clear idea of which tasks influence what results and which are key in 80/20 terms, are the only rational basis for deciding priorities. Give yourself this basis and you will be better equipped to work effectively both in terms of time spent on key issues, and of reducing or eliminating corresponding minor matters. But it is curiously difficult at one level to decide certain priorities. If we ask why, it brings us to the vexed question of the urgent versus the important.

The urgent and the important are different in nature. Yet both generate pressure to deal with them 'before anything else'. It may help to think here of four categories as shown in Fig. 5.1.

Urgent and important	Important but not urgent
Urgent but not important	Neither urgent nor important

Note: this is true of both planned and reactive tasks

Fig 5.1 Urgent vs. Important

Overall, the key is to think first and make considered decisions before letting particular circumstances push you into doing anything, or trying to do everything, first. Things that are to be actioned fast you must then either do, or delegate, at once; things that will wait should not just be put on one side, but planned or scheduled so that they get the time they deserve and then, in turn, get completed as appropriate.

This may seem difficult. It *is* difficult. But the difficulty is, at least in part, psychological. We do know what is most in need of action, certainly with hindsight, yet somehow the pressures of circumstances combine to give some things an 'unfair' advantage and we allow that to make the decision. This is a prime area where resolve is more important than technique, where there are no magic formulæ and making the right judgements in a considered way must become a habit if you are to remain organised in the face of such pressures.

That said, there are other ways of focusing attention and time on priorities and we look next at some examples. First, what about the bits and pieces? Can we adopt a useful approach to them? There are always matters that fall into such a category.

Make the miscellaneous a priority

Let me rephrase that heading: make the miscellaneous a priority *occasionally*. Nothing is perfect and it is inevitable that as you plan and sort and spend most time on priorities some of the small miscellaneous tasks may mount up. If this is realistically what happens – and for many people it is – then it is no good ignoring it and pretending that it does not occur. Rather you need to recognise it and decide on a way of dealing with it.

The best way is simply to programme an occasional blitz on the bits and pieces. Not because the individual things to do in this category are vital, but because clearing any backlog of this sort will act disproportionately to clear paper from your desk and systems. (Remember 80 per cent of the paper that crosses your desk is less important than the rest.) So, just occasionally clear a few minutes, or an hour if that is what it takes, and go through any outstanding bits and pieces. Write that name in your address book, answer that memo, phone back those people who you wish to keep in touch with but who have not qualified recently as priorities to contact, fill in that analysis form from accounts and all the rest of the kinds of thing you know tend to get left out and mount up.

Ideally there should be no bits and pieces. If you operate truly effectively then this sort of thing will not get left out. Pigs might fly. If you are realistic then, like me, you will find this useful. Be sure it does not happen too often, but when it does, you can take some satisfaction from the fact that a session to 'blitz on the bits' clears the decks and puts you back on top of things again making you more able to deal with the key things without nagging distractions.

Schedule – backwards

Some tasks are straightforward. They consist essentially of one thing and all that matters is deciding when to complete them and getting them done. But many tasks are made up of a number of stages which may be different things you do or do with other people. In addition, some stages may be conducted in different locations and the whole process may take days, weeks or months. All of which makes it important to schedule such multi-stage things in the right way if all priority tasks are to be completed on time. What can happen is that you take on a project and begin by feeling it is straightforward. Consider an example: you are to produce some sort of newsletter. Let us say it is in four stages: deciding the content, writing it, designing it and printing it. You complete stage one and stage two, but at this point it has taken somewhat longer than you thought. You hasten into stage three but halfway through it becomes clear that the complete job will not be finished on time. At that point it may be possible to speed things up, but other priorities could suffer, or the only way to hit the deadline may then be to use additional help, spend additional money or both. Fig. 5.2 shows graphically what is happening here.

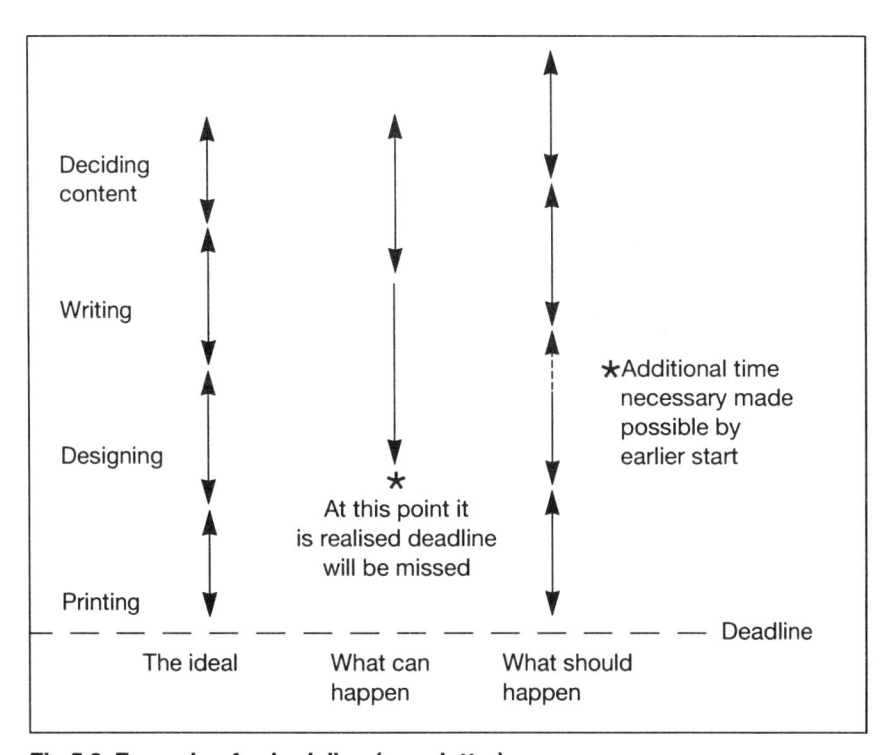

Fig 5.2 Example of scheduling (newsletter)

What needs to be done is to approach scheduling from the end of the cycle. Start with the deadline, estimate the time of each stage, make sure that the total job fits into the total time available and allow sufficient time for contingencies – things cannot always be expected to go exactly according to the book. Not only that, but do not look at the thing in isolation, see how it will fit in with or affect other current projects and responsibilities. It may be that you need to adjust the way stages work to fit with other matters that are in progress. For example, perhaps a certain stage can be delegated so that this is ready for you to pick up the project and take it through to the end. A number of options may be possible early on, whereas once you are part way through the options decline in number and the likelihood of other things being affected increases. All that is necessary here is that sufficient planning time precedes the project, and that in thinking it through you see the overall picture rather than judging whatever it is as a whole and oversimplifying it by just saying 'No problem'.

Be honest about deadlines

You must have heard the cry: 'If I had wanted it tomorrow I would have asked for it tomorrow'. The biggest problem about deadlines is their urgency – so many things seem to be wanted yesterday (partly no doubt because of someone's bad planning) that if you are not careful you spend your life running to keep up. As Alice (Through the Looking Glass) was told by the Red Queen: 'Now *here* you see it takes all the running you can do to stay in the same place. If you want to get somewhere else, you must run twice as fast as that.'

Deadlines must therefore be realistic, which was the burden of the point made in the previous section. Give yourself sufficient time, build in some contingency plans, and then you can deal with the thing properly and still be able to hit the deadline on time. Fine – or is it? There is another common complication to deadlines: people are dishonest about them. In some ways this is understandable – there may be a great deal hanging on a deadline being hit, and not only in terms of results but also of reputations. So what happens is that something must be done by the end of the month, so it is requested for the 25th 'to be on the safe side'. But this practice, and the people who do it, become known around an office and so the recipient of the deadline tells themself that a week later is fine. If several people are involved then the misjudgements can get worse as things are passed on and overall the chances of missing the date increase. It is ironic, but what starts out as a genuine attempt to ensure a deadline is met, ends up actually making it less likely that this will be done accurately.

The moral is clear. In any group with which you are associated, try to make sure the situation about deadlines is clear and open, and that everyone approaches the situation in the same way. If something needs completing on the 10th of the month, say so. If some contingency is sensible, again say so: 'This has to be with the client on 10th, let's aim to have it ready two days ahead of this to give time for a last check and make sure there is no chance of our failing to keep our promise to them'. This not only makes it more certain that the deadline involved will be hit, in part because people like it and commit to it more certainly, but also prevents other things being at risk because time is being spent chasing a deadline that is not, in fact, the real one. There is sufficient pressure in most offices without compounding the problem artificially. While many, many things have to be completed by a deadline (including writing this book), there are some where exactly how they are done affects how long they take. With these a review of methodology can pay dividends in saving time; with others such a review may allow the decision that they do not need actioning at all. And there may be more of these than you think. However, consider first those things that must be done but might be done differently from the way they are undertaken today.

Review task methodology

Another useful way to ensure you have adequate time for priority tasks is to review how exactly they, and other tasks too for that matter, are conducted. Clearly how you do something – the methodology – affects how long it takes. Because of this, there is sense in reviewing working methods on particular tasks and perhaps in doing so regularly. I am not suggesting that you stop all other work and spend time only on an examination of how things are done, but that you set yourself the job of reviewing a series of things over a period of time to search for worthwhile improvements.

Consider the example of my writing work again. The first book I wrote I drafted in long hand, my secretary typed it on a typewriter, I edited and made a great many changes to it and she retyped it, again some revision was necessary and the manuscript finally went off to the publishers. With this present title (appropriately enough!) my more recent way of working is more time efficient. I am inputting the material onto a word processor, editing somewhat as I go, and checking my less than perfect typing and spelling automatically with the spellchecker which is an inherent part of the system. I can then print a copy or do final editing on screen and the manuscript is off to the publisher that much more easily. I still have to decide what to write (I would not want the publisher to think it was too easy!) but the whole process takes much less time and even though I have had to learn to type – after a fashion – the time saving overall is still worthwhile and, of course, there are other advantages. For example, I can type on the move, on a journey for instance, and this saves still more time.

Obviously the changes that might be made to any task will depend on the nature of the task, but all sorts of things can be worthwhile, for example:

- systematising a task that was previously more random or circuitous
- changing actual methods (as with my example above)
- working with someone else (for example, again in my work, I do a little copywriting and brochure design, and always check the copy with one of my associates; another view focuses the process much more certainly and quickly than just thinking long and hard about it alone)
- lower standards: One method may achieve perfection, another – faster – one may achieve a lesser, but perfectly acceptable, result and sometimes save money
- sub-contract: in other words pay an external supplier to do something that they can do quicker, and sometimes cheaper and better, than you

Again such a list could go on and you may be able to think of routes to action that suit your particular job and work best for you. However, the principle of checking to see if there is a better way of doing something is sound. This needs *active* review and an open mind. Anything you can think of to prompt the process may be worth considering. Maybe if you select certain tasks and swap them with a colleague this will bring a fresh mind to bear and prompt new thinking about methodology; you do something for them and they for you. However it happens, make it happen, for there is never only one right way of doing anything for ever, and improved methodology can be a great time saver.

Eliminate the unnecessary

Most people will deny, if asked, that they spend time doing things that are unnecessary; after all it seems absurd. But it does happen. And it happens for all sorts of reasons. Consider a few examples:

- *Habit:* you have always attended a monthly meeting, read a regularly circulated report, checked certain information, filed certain items and kept in touch with certain people. And it is easy for things to run on, repeating automatically without thought and for such things to take up time unnecessarily.
- *Insurance:* you do things for protective reasons. In case something goes wrong, in case someone asks why, in case ... what? Sometimes the reason is not clear, there is just a feeling that it is safer to do something than not. Filing and documenting things are examples of this.
- *Avoidance:* the real reason for something to be done long disappeared, but continuing to do it means you have no time – and excuse – to take on or try out something new and perhaps risky. Be honest, have you really never put off doing something new?
- *Expectation:* you do things not because of their real worth, but because it is, or you feel it is, expected of you. In a team environment you do not want to let others down, though you will let down things more by ignoring priorities.
- *Appearances:* you do things because they are 'good things' to be involved with, perhaps politically, and every organisation has some politics. Your position and perception around the organisation is important, but you must not overdo this kind of involvement, not least because it can become self defeating, being seen as an ego trip by someone who has nothing better to do.

All of these and more may occur and, make no mistake, there are no doubt valid reasons under each heading – you really do need to attend some meetings simply to demonstrate commitment and this is a tangible and priority result. But . . . but, this is an area to address very hard. Are there any things you are doing that you can stop doing without affecting the results significantly? For most people an honest appraisal shows the answer to be 'yes', so such a review both immediately if you have not done so for a while, and regularly to ensure that unnecessary tasks are not creeping in again, is very worthwhile. How is this done? Very simply (it is something consultants like me spend a lot of time doing with their clients), you ask *why*? Why is something being done? And if the answer is because that is the way it is, that is the system, or, worst of all, that is the way it has always been done, then ask again. If you can really not find a better reason then the task may well be a candidate for elimination. Failing that, maybe you can do it less often, in less detail or otherwise adjust the approach to save time and allow attention to the priorities. This is another area that can start from the time log, it is not just what you are doing that matters, but the time it takes. If you are ruthless about this kind of questioning and honest about the answers then time may be saved in this way.

One particular kind of task may very sensibly be categorised as unnecessary, at least to you. Black holes, collapsed stars so massive and with such powerful gravity that they pull in everything and even light cannot escape from them, make the old expression about going down the plug hole seem pretty small beer. In most offices there are corporate equivalents of this phenomenon, 'black hole jobs' that suck in all the time you can think of and more. Watch out for them and beware – just like real black holes, if you get too near there is no going back and an involvement means all your other plans have to be put on hold.

What kind of jobs warrant this description? They are usually projects involving a number of different tasks, they are often contentious, may involve an impossibility of pleasing everyone and can be ruinous of reputations, as well as taking up a quite disproportionate amount of time. They include a range of things from organising the organisation's twentieth anniversary party and celebrations to moving the company to new offices. Such things have to be done (you may have such things in your job description, in which case it is a different matter), but they often call for 'volunteers'. This can mean the Managing Director suggests it, in public, in a way that makes refusal risky: 'It is only a suggestion, of course, but do bear in mind who's making it'. At this point others heave sighs of relief and resolve not even to get involved in a tiny support role.

You will know, if you have any wits at all, the kind of tasks in your office that have these characteristics and should, if you value your ability to keep on top of your other tasks, plan to be well away whenever there is a danger of you getting lumbered with one. Do not say you have not been warned.

Finally, a last word on priorities.

Be confident of your priorities

The best time managers organise successfully to concentrate time and energy on their priorities and one reason they do so seems to be an ability to make prompt and firm decisions about what they should be. Others use up hours of valuable time not only deciding what should come first, but reviewing the decision again and again to double check it. Of course, circumstances change and some ongoing review may be necessary but it does not help, as the saying has it, to keep digging up the plant to look at the roots to see if it is growing well. Similarly the constant reassurance some seem to seek in their decisions may just waste time and is also, in my view, a certain route to stress.

The process starts with review and analysis. As you can only do one thing at a time – so important a fact that I make no apology for repeating it – you must be clear what the key factors on your list are and which are in fact most important, and constitute the real priorities. Having considered all sides of this thoroughly, you need to make a decision. There is no reason at that point to doubt that it is other than a good one. And, in any case, no amount of further review will change the fact that you can do only one thing at a time, and however illogical, it is this that a long list of things to do sometimes prompts us to look to change. It does not matter whether the first thing to be done is followed on the list by ten more or a hundred more, something has to be done first.

So make the decision, stick to it, and get on with the task. The quicker you do that the sooner you will be able to move on down the list. Much is written about stress in the work place (though not by me).

Stress is a reaction to circumstances rather than the circumstances themselves. Being able to say that:

- you know your priorities
- you have made work planning decisions sensibly, based on reasonable and thorough consideration of all the facts
- you are sure there is no more, for the moment, you can do to make things easier
- you know that as you proceed with the task you are going to do it effectively and that the methodology you will use makes sense

should allow you to be comfortable about the process, and to reject any tendency to stress. While trying to work at something while worried that there may be greater priorities, knowing that a variety of other things are queuing up for attention but are as yet unsorted, and having any doubts about the way you are doing things, is a sure recipe for stress. Keep calm by keeping organised and you will be better placed to maintain and increase your effectiveness.

Getting your priorities clear is not an area to be underestimated. Give it a try, look at your time log, analyse what you do and you may find with some initial horror that there are quite a number of things that you do that can be left undone without causing any problem. That horror, which is in any case about the past, can then turn to looking creatively at how to use the time saved. But what about the actions that are necessary? There is one common factor amongst them all: any kind of action tends to generate paper, and more paper and more . . . sorry, it is a problem of which we are all too well aware. It is the subject of handling paperwork that is taken up in the next chapter.

6

Controlling the paperwork
Making paperwork productive

'You see things; and say "Why?" But I dream things that never were; and say "Why not?"'

GEORGE BERNARD SHAW

Let us start on a positive note. Paperwork need not overpower you. You can keep it under control, though you may not be able to eliminate it altogether. It is necessary, or certainly some of it is, and here we are ten years after the IT experts began to talk about the 'paperless office' and there still seems to be as much as ever on my desk. Letters, memos, faxes, reports, forms, proposals, and more all combine to create a steady stream of paperwork across your desk. If you are not reading things you are writing them, and if you are not doing that you are processing things that involve paperwork. All this can take up a significant proportion of your working day. In time management terms the job is to eliminate it, or minimise it, and process what must be there promptly and efficiently.

This chapter consists primarily of a range of ideas, large and small, that can help you keep the paperwork under control. It is not exhaustive, no such review could be, and the ideas are as important as examples of a way of thinking about how papers should be dealt with as they are in themselves. Ultimately, because what constitutes the papers on any individual's desk is unique, we must all find our own solutions to this problem. The principles here, however, are selected to provide a suitable foundation for that basis. And as good a place as any to start is with some thoughts about minimising the volume of paper you deal with day to day.

Aim to minimise paperwork

Perhaps the first thing to ask in this area is simply: is all your paperwork really necessary? Let it be clear straight away, much of it will be.

This book itself has already recommended that your work/time plan is in writing to give only one example. But some paperwork can be eliminated, and often all that is necessary, before you put pen to paper or start to dictate, is that you pause for a second and ask yourself whether what you are about to do is really necessary. Have a look at what is on your desk, see how much of it was not really necessary, think how much of it could achieve its aims in some other way. Yet someone is sending all this to your desk and is presumably well intentioned in so doing. Perhaps much of what you create on paper is similarly regarded.

So, what do you do about it? The key alternative to written communication is *the telephone*; it is usually much quicker to lift the telephone than to write something, and, as not everything needs a written record, this is one of the surest ways of reducing paperwork.

It is also worth a note here about the now ubiquitous *fax*. It is not so much the sense of urgency this bestows on things which interests us here (though it is undeniably useful), it is the style. It seems to be that an altogether less formal style has developed for the fax. It is one that is perfectly acceptable internally around a big organisation with a number of offices, and with people in other organisations, as a quick form of communication where brevity is of the essence. A small point here: remember to take a copy of any fax you wish to keep that arrives on thermal paper as this fades quite quickly and you may well then waste time later tracking down invisible addresses or other details.

Two other points are worth a mention. The first, in the interests of slowing the destruction of forests to make paper, as much as time, is copies. It is one thing to write to someone, but it is the circulation of copies that feeds the proliferation of paperwork as much as anything. Think before you list half the company; who *really* needs a copy? Secondly, can it be standardised? There may be a number of routine communications that can be recorded in the word processor – either whole letters or documents or separate paragraphs that can be used to put together something suitable. Here technology really does save time. But there is one very important caveat here. Never, never use standard material if it is inappropriate. In the sales area, for example, I see many letters and proposals which shout 'standard' when they should be seen as an individual response to the individual customer who receives them. Further, any standard material should be double checked to see that it is well written. Otherwise, by definition, something poor or, at worst, damaging may be sent out hundreds of times a month. It can certainly save time but should not do so at the cost of an unacceptable reduction in quality.

Make a habit of brevity

Your written communication will be less time consuming if it is not only brief but, choosing my words carefully, succinct and precise and, of course, clear (this is not the place for a treatise on making communications understandable, but communication should never be assumed to be easy; it is often the reverse, and misunderstandings must be responsible for a massive amount of wasted time as things are queried and clarified). This is worth a short (sic) point here because I notice many people have a curious reluctance to write short business letters. An example makes the point: A writes to B prior to a meeting asking when his flight arrives and whether he would like to be met at the airport. So often the reply will be along the lines of:

'Dear Mr A
Thank you for your kind letter of 24 July 1993 about my forthcoming visit to your offices next week on Thursday 30 July. I am pleased to say that all my travel arrangements are now complete – you may remember I was having trouble with one of the connections – and I now have full details. I arrive on Flight 915 at 10.00 am. This should suit our lunch meeting well and not make any problem with the timing.

With regard to your kind offer to meet me, perhaps I could say how grateful I would be for your assistance in this regard . . .'

And so on.

If the two know each other even a little, surely there can be nothing wrong with something that says:

'Dear Mr A
It was good to hear from you. I arrive on Flight 915 at 10.00 am on 30 July. It would be a great deal help to be met at the airport; I will look out for your driver.
Many thanks, I look forward to seeing you soon.
Yours . . .'

I know which I would prefer to receive: the second. The information is clear, I do not have to wade through any extraneous material, it saves me time, and may well be one third or one quarter of the length of the first one. And it took less time to write and get sent. I think it is still perfectly polite and I wish more people adopted just this kind of approach. If it can be said in three lines then say it in three lines.

Now consider the time saving of three page memos reduced to one, reports of ten page instead of 20 . . . but I promised this would be a short paragraph. Enough said; point made.

Minimal memos

The well known memo makes up a major part of the paperwork in many offices. In the last paragraph I made a plea for brevity; here is a simple idea that can save even more time. Assume you receive a memo – a full page of some colleague's meanderings no doubt – and what it says, in a word, is: Can you attend a meeting of the planning committee at 3.00 pm this coming Friday. Assume that you can and are prepared to attend. Now all you need to do is photocopy the memo that came to you, write on it 'TO:-' at the top and ring the name of the original sender, write 'FINE, SEE YOU THERE' at the bottom and sign it. If you really want to be rash with time, take an extra second and add a ring round your message to highlight it (a red pen does this nicely). Then send it back.

Excuse a touch of sarcasm here, but one so often sees people laboriously preparing typed and sometimes over long memos when this kind of procedure will do very well; some companies have preprinted sheets for their memos that are designed to take a reply.

A final thought: in such circumstances you can always telephone, though consider who it is and how long they will chat and whether they would appreciate confirmation in writing for the record.

> **NOTICE**
>
> **Use the Bulletin Board**
>
> Another quick time saver that can usefully apply to certain kinds of communication (and not others) is to make use of the Bulletin Board. If your office – company or department – does not have one, get one soon, and then make it clear to people that certain things will not be circulated widely at great cost (you can specify the categories of information in advance). A brief notice posted once can save time and it quickly becomes a habit for people to look (though I know one company where they have a 'Spot the deliberate mistake competition' with a prize to encourage people to look). Worth a try.

Minimise your paper handling

Here is an interesting experiment you can try (it will not take long and could end up saving you time). Select ten or so items that come across your desk today, a mixture of letters, memos and documents all of which demand some action on your part and mark them all with a red spot in the top right-hand corner. Then simply deal with them as normal. And every time you touch them thereafter add another red spot to the top right-hand corner. As time passes you will then produce a count of how many times things go through your hands. For example, a letter arrives today and you read it (1), you decide not to deal with it immediately but put it with a job on which you intend to spend time in the afternoon (2). In the afternoon you make a start, work out what needs to be done but are interrupted (3). The letter joins a number of items that overlap the day and you pick it up again the following morning (4). And so it goes on. In this case we are imagining just a simple letter. In other cases projects and processes have been referred to which span weeks or months; you can imagine the incidence of red spots.

This is known as the 'measles test'. And it can help you identify how your way of handling things affects the time that dealing with them takes. Sometimes the multiple 'spotting' is necessary, but other cases may well surprise you because you had no idea just how often some things cross your desk before they are resolved. The first step to change is always knowing where change should be applied. The information gained in this way will be useful. Sometimes improvement is easy, for example the use of a Prompt File (see page 52) will cure some 'spotting', in other cases it may lead you to a review of your method of handling certain tasks. In any event, you should adopt the principle of trying to handle things the minimum number of times before they are resolved.

If you have a clear plan and a system for categorising your work then things should be dealt with immediately, or held for some reason and then dealt with. If this is applied rigorously then the time taken up by papers being handled many times will be reduced. But again let us be realistic. Most jobs are not, in fact, made up of thousands of completely separate tasks, though it would perhaps be easier if they were. For many people there are a great many links between different items and areas; indeed an element of some jobs involves creatively seeing links that can be turned into opportunities, and with the process of what is called synergy (or colloquially the 2+2=5 effect). All of this may demand sufficient review of the situations represented by your paperwork for this opportunity process to be possible. So this rule, like some others, must not be applied slavishly. You need sufficient sight of some items to operate effectively and must be careful not to reduce paper handling in a way you feel does not suit or work well in your individual job.

I have no wish to create a straitjacket for readers with anything I suggest. However, the principle advocated here is sound and as a general rule being aware of how many times things go through your hands and trying to keep that number down makes good sense in time terms.

Do not let files and filing waste time

I once saw a cartoon which showed a picture of a world weary looking secretary standing by a manager's desk. She was holding a bundle of papers and the caption depicted her saying: 'Do you want this again – or shall I file it?' And there, it seems to me, is the problem of filing in a nutshell. Too often it is used simply as a way of getting paper off the desk, and while there is some sort of system to suggest where papers go, there is no real thought about just what should be kept, or for how long, and it is this that wastes time. One of the most frightening statistics to emerge from any survey of business practice was that from one multinational giant which showed that only 10 per cent of the papers put into filing were ever referred to again; this in an organisation proud of its efficiency – what hope for ordinary mortals?

This means that 90 per cent could have been destroyed, and the cost of 'keeping them at the right temperature in comfortable surroundings', as the survey called it, is enormous. The time, our consideration here, is equally worrying. But some things do need to be filed, so you cannot throw the baby out with the bath water; you need a system.

By all means let a secretary design or help with the design of a system, but to achieve consistency you should always decide what goes where. Do the papers about that reorganisation go under R for reorganisation, O for organisation or office, E for efficiency drive, or B for Boss's Pet Projects? There are often serious problems here as anyone who has tried to locate a file, say, a year old, knows; few have memories that will hold this kind of detail for ever. So get the system right. It is difficult to generalise, you may need Account files, Project files or a dozen more; or all of these. It is usually better to have a number of categories, each A–Z, rather than one giant system that has to cope with everything. I once saw complete muddle caused in such a system because one unthinking filing clerk put everything marked 'FILE' under F!

As you review potential filing material you only really have three options for action:

- do not file it, throw it away; and in the light of the statistics above this is to be seriously considered
- file it with no thought for how long it will stay there
- file it with a clear indication of a destroy date (or at least a review date)

Let me prompt you to think carefully about how much you need to keep things and then review some ways of keeping filing under control. Consider what is on or around your desk at present. How much of it could you throw away right now? Probably the answer is very little. But imagine those same papers in the future, how many of them will you need in six months, in a year, in two years? Here the honest answer will be less and getting fewer as you go into the future. So why not throw more away?

Think about where else things are held. If you need to check something in, say, a regular financial summary only once in three months, why even have a file on it if you know your secretary can get it from the accountant in 30 seconds? Think about the things you hold just in case. In your heart you probably know you are not at all bad at judging what will be required, yet you still keep too much. Trust your instincts, remember the old saying: if it looks like a duck and quacks, then it probably *is* a duck. If you are 99 per cent sure it is going to be rubbish very soon, you are probably right, after all, they are your papers. So throw it away.

But if you are wrong and need something you have thrown away that may do more than waste time, so consider some insurance. Here are two systems that will act in this way:

- *Batch filing:* this is where filing is *not* done too early. Everything is put in simple A–Z order in a batch file and only filed after, say, a month (you pick the time). But before it is filed you look through it to see what you still want to keep. After even one month you might be surprised how much you ditch.

- *the 'Chron' file:* this system works by filing an extra copy of every letter and document produced for you in straight A–Z date order in something like a large lever arch file. This is kept for a fixed length of time, maybe a year in quarterly files to make it more manageable. Every time the fourth quarter file is full, the first quarter file is thrown away and you start a new quarter file with the current material.

Either or both may suit you. They let you be a lot more ruthless in throwing paper away, because on the odd occasion you are proved wrong you can find it in the back up file.

Many systems benefit from a destroy system. This can be done by setting dates (perhaps in year batches) or even very simply by capacity. I have one file, kept in date order, which works by throwing something out of the drawer every time something new is added. The drawer is always just on full, and this corresponds well with how long the contents appear to remain useful and no one has to waste any time over it.

This area must be systemised on a basis that works for your office. If things are well ordered, if you can find what you want (and this is inherently easier if there is not so much in total to find it amongst) and do not have to spend time constantly re-sorting the system to make room for more and more, then it will work well and you will run it and not it run you. Order in the filing must save time.

Keep papers neat

I like to think that I never lose things (well rarely – or my secretary will edit this out). But on the last two of those rare occasions, in both cases I discovered the lost paper caught under a paper clip hidden at the back of a batch of correspondence which was about something quite different. It is a small point perhaps, but you can waste some time hunting for papers and re-collating papers that have got out of order in this sort of way. Paper clips are not the best way to keep papers tidy. Beware – they do tend to trap other items and catch you unawares.

But papers must be kept tidy. Do not keep too much together (it becomes unmanageable), and worry in particular about files and papers that travel about with you both around and out of the office. Staple them, punch them or bind them rather than use paper clips, and experiment with whatever sort of files – and there are many different styles – suit you. I favour the sort that have a small top and bottom flap to hold things all round and elastic bands that snap across the corners. The more things you have to work on in parallel the more your current papers need organising neatly. If you only get one file out at a time and work on that until it is neatly replaced by something else, then it is less of a problem. If you are paid to keep many balls in the air at once, then it is vital. Time management is, in this respect, similar to juggling. If there are a lot of balls in the air and one is dropped, more tend to follow. The more you have on the go, the greater the disruption and waste of time if something becomes disorganised. Keep papers physically under control.

Computerise it – but carefully

It has become one of the great twentieth-century myths that computers will transform office work, and make everything fast and efficient to action. But like other great promises ('Our cheque is in the post') it is not entirely to be trusted. Now I have nothing against computers and there are things that one cannot now imagine working any other way. And yet . . . there are questions, certainly as far as efficiency and time utilisation are concerned, at desk level for the individual executive.

There are examples of things now available that manifestly work well:

- computerised databases that can be accessed on a desk top PC and which dramatically reduce the time needed to sort through, analyse or communicate with those names on them
- graphics programs that can turn a set of confusing figures into a graph that can impart a key point in a moment
- desk top publishing (DTP) which means documentation can be produced in-house at the touch of a button, removing the need to liaise with three separate outside suppliers
- electronic mail that can communicate with a branch office for you, *and* let you peep in their files
- computerised versions of things like drawing diagrams, analysing figures, interpreting statistics (and playing noughts and crosses!) which make their manual equivalents look positively quaint.

You can probably think of many more. Some you will use and regard as routine, and many can save time. Yet there are systems that for all their cleverness do not fit their role so well. Think of some of the systems you may be frustrated by as a customer, in the bank, with an insurance company or hotel. Take an hotel account as an example. They are, one presumes, efficient for the hotel but many are very difficult to fathom without a degree in abbreviations. It is customer service that has suffered in this case. So there is another side to computers; you need expert help to set up many systems (and in some cases to operate them), there is a high capital cost though this is coming down, and they are all too readily used as an excuse for *not* doing things (if I had a small coin for every time I have heard someone in a travel agents say: 'Sorry, the computer is down', I could travel round the world free). Above all, in the context of our topic here, they take time to set up and the equation of time must be carefully balanced to see what makes best sense.

A friend of mine recently got an 'electronic organiser'. He spent every evening for a week entering every telephone number, every account number and reference from his bank account to his diary. As far as he was concerned a new age had dawned. A week later he had pressed a wrong button or something and all the information was lost. So, especially if you are not in the generation that has grown up with all this, tread carefully. There are things in this area that are great time savers. There are also pitfalls, costly in time, for the unwary. By all means use what you can, check out new things as they become available, but consider the alternatives as well and you may conclude some of them still hold good. If you can find that telephone number faster just by turning it up in a pocket notebook, why not do just that until something comes along that really is better for you?

Do not duplicate information unnecessarily

There is a time expenditure in keeping up any information system. More so if the information is being recorded in identical or similar form in several different places. This is worth a check, and there is a quick check you can run in a few moments. The job you do will give rise to the areas of information with which you are concerned, but an example and Fig. 6.1 will demonstrate.

Such an analysis will quickly show the extent of any kind of duplication – and the sheer extent of the recording going on. If you then think about where information is most often sought, you may well find that only a minority of places originally listed are highlighted. This in turn poses questions about the other places where the information appears. How many of them can be scrapped or reduced. Time and neglect, or if you want to feel better about it, concentration on other matters, allows a proliferation of systems and information over time, sometimes far beyond what is really useful at present. Incidentally, another area to watch is computer information systems in which the technical ability to include extra information is often sufficient reason for it to be included. It is the use that is made of such sources that is important.

Do not proliferate information unnecessarily

Sometimes tasks seem important and then something happens which shows that this was not true at all, or perhaps not true any more. One thing that sometimes happens is that time is wasted because once something is originated then thinking about it ceases. An experience of mine will illustrate this. In one company where I did some work I asked if they had certain information (certain sales analysis, but the subject is not important). At first the answer was that they did not, then someone in the sales office said that they in fact sent such a breakdown to the Managing Director's office each month. The Managing Director denied all knowledge of this, but his secretary, overhearing the request, said she held a file of the information.

	1	2	3	4	5	6
A	X	X	X	X	X	X
B	X		X	X		
C	X	X			X	
D	X	X		X		X
E	X		X			X

← Information

↑ Record system

Note: Matching where information is recorded with how it is usually accessed will produce savings. For example, if information 4 is usually looked for in system A: does it need to be in B and D?

Fig. 6.1 Checking for duplicated information

We checked and there it was. It arrived on her desk each month and she filed it. On tracking this back we discovered that some two years previously the Managing Director had asked for this special analysis and a summary for that month had been produced. He had looked at it and put it in his secretary's filing tray, and she had opened a file for it. The sales office produced it again the next month, sent it to the MD's office, but his secretary filed it without showing it to him. This had then been repeated every month for two years! It took someone in the sales office several hours each month to complete the work to produce the figures, and, after the first time, it had all been a complete waste.

Such situations continue all too easily once the initial moment has passed. Just who was at fault? The sales office, the MD, the secretary? All of them? It just happened they might say, but more to the point could it have been prevented? You should make a rule that whenever you are asked or need to provide any information to anyone (with copies to whomever else), you make a diary note to check at some time in the future – in six or 12 months perhaps – whether it is still necessary. Find out whether it still needs to be sent:

- on the same frequency (would quarterly be as good as monthly?)
- to all the listed people?
- in as much detail (would some sort of summary do?)

Any change that will save time is worthwhile and you may find that it is simply not necessary any more. Very few people will *ask* for information to stop coming to them, but if asked may well admit that they can happily do without it. Be wary of this sort of thing, or it is quite possible that all around your organisation things will be repeated unnecessarily.

Do not put it in writing

I felt for the course delegate who told me that a 20-page report he had been asked to prepare had been handed back by the manager to whom he presented it with a request for a verbal summary. While he had lavished care and attention on the report, he was unprepared for this and his spur of the moment presentation was not as fluent as he would have wished, the matter to which the report referred was dropped and the report was never read (it was no doubt filed rather than destroyed). He was naturally aggrieved and resented the incident – with some cause perhaps.

Certainly management ought to consider the consequences of its action, decisions and requests to others in time terms. What avoids something taking up time for you may land someone else with a great deal of extra work. If you are a manager, your responsibility for good time utilisation covers the team. It is little good being productive yourself if everyone else is tied up with all sorts of unnecessary tasks and paperwork. Jobs need to be done, action taken, consideration given and in many cases written instructions, guidelines or confirmation are not simply necessary, they are vital. But on other occasions that may well not be the case. The report referred to above should, in all likelihood, not have been requested. Certainly the action, or lack of it, was decided upon without the detail documented in the report being looked at, and presumably the manager concerned felt he had enough information to make a valid decision. This kind of thing can often happen. Time may be wasted unless the instigator of such action thinks first and only specifies written details of something if it is really necessary. Similarly, those in receipt of such requests should not be afraid to ask, and check whether such exercises are really necessary. Whichever category of person you are in, and it may well be both, give it a thought. Of course, there are other considerations. If you just say 'Shan't' next time the Managing Director asks for a report, do not come crying to me if you are read the riot act. But in many circumstances a check can and should be made (even with the MD) and less paper is put about as a result.

Write faster

Now 'Write faster' may seem in the same category of advice as maxims such as 'Save water, shower with a friend', and you may well ask what you are supposed to do – rush through things so that you either write rubbish or no one can read your writing if you are writing in longhand? Neither – the point I want to make concerns the quality of writing. Think of the last reasonably complicated document you had to write, a report perhaps. You had to think about what to say, and designing the structure and sequence of the message and content of this may have taken a little time. Incidentally, you will do this job quicker if you make some notes, it is amazing how many people simply launch into such tasks and then have to redraft what they produce because it becomes a muddle – but I digress. You then had to decide *how* you would put it. Many people are hesitant in such tasks and find that because they are uncertain of how to phrase things they proceed slowly, with much pause for thought.

Writing is a skill like many others used in business, and it can be improved by study. When my career began to involve me in more and longer, more complicated writing, first reports and proposals and later books, I began to take an interest in writing style. I read some books, acquired some reference books and went on a course. I found it interesting (my previous education had had no special bias in this direction) and I found it useful. Some years later, I would still not claim to be the best writer in the world, but I know I write better than in the past.

So far so good. The time I had spent had certainly been worthwhile; but I then discovered there was another benefit. I was writing faster. None of this meant that I no longer had to consider what I wrote, and I had not suddenly accelerated out of sight as it were, but the increase was noticeable and useful; it saved me time. Other people have confirmed my experience and I have no reason not to think that there is not a useful potential benefit here available to many. Fluent written communication is an important business skill in any case. If you can learn to improve the standard to which you write and gain a bonus in time saved over the rest of your career as well then some study is well worthwhile.

As a start, the boxed paragraph sets out a systematic approach to the drafting of any document. It may appear to be over engineering the process, but it works and produces better quality documentation – in less time.

A SYSTEMATIC APPROACH TO WRITING WELL AND QUICKLY

Do not just start writing at the beginning and work your way through. It will, in the end, be much quicker to plan out the content and then 'fill in' the detail. A sequence such as the following works well:

(i) *Listing:* list all the points involved, anything and everything that may need to be included, literally at random over a page. Do not worry about length, sequence, grouping topics or anything else – just note the points to be covered. This is sometimes referred to as 'mind mapping'.

(ii) *Sorting:* this should put the key points in sequence (perhaps by numbering in a second colour rather than rewriting). Delete any points that will not be worth space, keep thinking of anything else that needs to go in.

(iii) *Arranging:* next produce from what you have noted a more detailed synopsis or writing plan. This should list all the headings, subheadings and notes to yourself about what must be covered under each, in sequence, reasonably comprehensively but in headline form.

(iv) *Draft:* then draft the complete text, following the headings, to create the complete report or other document. It is often better not to try to perfect this as you go along, but to get everything down and then review it in the next stage.

(v) *Edit:* now check over and finalise what you have got down. Do not worry if you are not word perfect first time – few people are – the rule here is edit, edit and, if necessary, edit again (the time spent will link to the importance of the document). Remember, if it is designed to prompt some action (get agreement to a plan of action, perhaps) and fails to do so, far more time may then be taken up than would ever have been needed on a final edit to ensure it was better put, or more persuasive, in the first place.

The more complex and longer the document the better this will work (though do not underestimate the length of document that needs this approach); it was the way this book started. This systematic approach will produce better documents than a more ad hoc approach, and save time, creating in the process the habit of systematically writing in this way that is a career asset.

A short document and things we know well are not difficult or time consuming to create. But longer documents can be, and as well as reducing the amount of paperwork in an office, we want to streamline it, and if you can put longer documents together more quickly this will help.

Lastly in this chapter, though by no means the least in terms of potential use, some thoughts on an absurdly simple yet effective time saver. No prizes for guessing to what the next heading refers.

The most time saving object in your office

Finally in this section, although it was touched on under the section on filing on page 92, the nature of office paperwork is such that it is only right to end by returning to the simple premise of throwing things away. The WPB is, of course, the Waste Paper Basket. It helps efficiency and time if your desk and office are tidy, if what you need is neatly and accessibly placed – a place for everything and everything in its place – but not if such good order is submerged under sheer quantity of paper, most of it of a 'just in case' nature.

All sorts of things cross your desk: magazines, direct mail, items marked 'To read and circulate' and 'For information', copies of things that are of no real relevance to you and minutes of meetings that you wish had never taken place. Much of this pauses for far too long, creating heaps and extra filing trays and bundles in your brief case (things to read at home, for instance). It is better to deal with things early rather than later. When it has mounted up it is always going to be more difficult to get through, and an immediate decision will keep the volume down, for example:

- if you are on a circulation list and do not want to look at something today, then add your name further down the list and pass it on; it will get back to you later when you may be less busy
- at least check a magazine at once, maybe you can tear out an article or two and throw the rest away
- consider very carefully whether the vast plethora of things that 'might be useful' are, in fact, ever likely to be, either file them or throw them away

All these kinds of thinking and action help, but most people are conservative and reluctant to throw things away. Unless you are very untypical there will be things on and around your desk right now that could be thrown out. Have a look, and, as you look, do some throwing. Make a full WPB a target for the end of the day. Imagine it has a scale running down the inside to show how full it is. This scale could almost be graduated, not in volume, but in minutes saved.

With the means to get the paper more under control (remember perfection may not be possible), we can move on to another essential of the world of the organisation: people. Like them or not, interactions between them certainly take up some time. For many this is where most time goes, and it is the subject of the next chapter.

7

People and management
Working with and controlling others

'A man is known by the company he organises".
AMBROSE BIERCE

You will encounter people of all sorts throughout business. Some you will get on with, some you will not; some will help you, inform you, or teach you; some will infuriate you; some you will work with, getting things done that would not occur, or occur so well, otherwise – but, male or female, young or old, senior or junior – all will waste your time. Some will do so intentionally, others unwittingly, but it will happen. What is more, because people interactions in business are vital, there is no way of avoiding them, but you have to work with them in a way that anticipates and minimises the disruptive effect they can have on your time. Here we look at a range of topics, useful in themselves, and as examples of the approach to take, that help. Some will be most appropriate if you manage other people, others are more generally applicable; all will save you time.

This chapter is arranged in three main sections so as to deal first with general 'people matters' then with issues most appropriate if you manage others and last with matters relating particularly to when people come together – that great potential time waster – meetings. There is inevitably, intentionally, some overlap as that is the way things work in real life:

1 PEOPLE ISSUES

The intention here is to give the feel of a whole range of 'people issues' that can affect the utilisation of time either positively or negatively. The first few points may perhaps be considered general or background, the gain by handling them well can, however, be considerable. Certainly the first is a case in point.

Socialising and informal contact

An organisation is a club, colleagues are acquaintances or friends and work can be fun (not all the time perhaps, but it is a relevant objective), and this makes for problems as, for example, 'Good morning' turns into half the morning disappearing in chatter. It is an area where a time log may provide surprising information.

Now I am not suggesting that all social contact is forbidden, perish the thought. I like a chat and a nice piece of gossip as much as anyone, indeed without some of this to foster relationships, an organisation would not only be a duller place but a less effective one. There is an indefinable dividing line between the social chat and the business content, and curtailing anything we cannot definitely label 'Business' will risk throwing the baby out with the bath water.

On the other hand you do need to keep things in proportion, curtail excesses and watch out for those moments at which the danger is greatest that time will be really wasted. These include:

- first thing in the morning, when greetings tend to turn into an in-depth analysis of the meal, date, TV or movie, sporting event or disaster of the previous evening
- breaks, when the coffee comes round or people gather around the drinks machine
- lunch, when even the process of discussing when to go, with whom, and where assumes time consuming proportions
- the end of the day when everyone is getting tired and a chat is a welcome excuse to wind down early.

There are places too where you are prone to get caught and conversation runs on. In some companies Reception acts as a sort of plaza with people coming and going through it in different directions using their passing each other as an excuse for a chat. Every office layout has its own version of this. Because people's work patterns are different, moments when you have time for a chat may not suit others and vice versa. There needs to be mutual respect for people's time and concentration around an office, and everyone can play a part in fostering such a culture. For example, an earlier section (on page 45) advocated taking an occasional break to aid concentration. Do not, however, use these to break in on other people. Not only does this waste their time, but what you intended to be a two minute pause may very easily turn into half an hour, two cups of coffee and, even if some of the conversation is useful, a major disruption of two people's schedules.

So beware and be careful – there is no need to be stand-offish and there is particularly no need to screen out the useful conversations, but remember that this is a major factor eating away at productivity, and act accordingly.

On the other hand you do need to see and talk to people. But, like so much else, how and when this is organised should be a conscious plan, one conditioned not least by the time that will be taken up. How do you approach this? This has become a technique in its own right, with its own abbreviation: MBWA. These initials stand for 'Management By Walking About', a phrase coined, I think, in the bestselling business book *In Search of Excellence*, Thomas J. Peters and Robert H. Waterman Jnr, Harper and Row, and it describes the need for management, perhaps especially senior management, to keep in touch at a direct and personal level with the other departments and people with whom they work. However good the management control systems that exist in an organisation, there is no substitute for going and seeing and hearing for yourself what is going on, what the problems are and what opportunities are present.

Management can very often become protected and cloistered to the point that it has no genuine feel for how other parts of the organisation work. So not only is this sound advice, but it is a real aid to communication, and it can also save time. At its most dramatic, one fact finding walk-about can negate the need for several meetings and a report as the evidence of your own eyes and ears jumps you ahead in the decision making process. Being in touch makes a real difference to your ability to operate, so the balance of time here – taken and saved – is likely to be productive.

This is especially true if you can find ways of creating opportunities for this that serve more than one purpose. I was given a good example of this when I broke off writing this text for a couple of days to conduct a short course for a client company. The Managing Director both introduced the programme and came back to round things off at the end.

This is, I believe, good practice, demonstrating a senior management commitment to what others are being asked to give up time for and generally supporting a training culture. At the end of the second day drinks were available and at one moment as everyone was chatting, the Managing Director interrupted his discussion with one of his people to make a note – they had stumbled on a useful point and he noted it for later follow up. This can happen quite naturally as the chat mixes with more serious comment.

The point here, made clear to me when the others had left, was that the Managing Director, who was doubtless a busy man, consciously saw such a gathering as serving a double purpose: he was happy to support training, but more ready to do so if it provided an opportunity for some of the 'walking about' he felt was anyway necessary. He might have considered just giving an introduction (with no feedback and only contributing to the training) as not being time well spent, but the addition of drinks and discussion – in fact taking longer – made it serve two purposes and become well worthwhile. An appropriate example to appear at an appropriate moment.

Making a working lunch work

An army, it is said, marches on its stomach. In business too we all have to pause now and then for fuel, as it were. Indeed in some parts of the world food is altogether more important than fuel (in Singapore, for example, I am always told it is the national sport, and am inclined to believe it). That apart, there are a couple of practical things to be said about it.

First, consider the phrase 'business lunch'. For most people this conjures up something expensive, lengthy, and substantial. If you add in the time taken to get to such an event, then the total time involved is something to be considered very carefully. You need to think about whether to accept such invitations, or how often to do so. You may need to meet with the person concerned, but there may be other ways to achieve this. And you certainly need to think twice before you issue such invitations yourself. Again the first question is whether a meeting is necessary, then whether it needs to be at lunch. Entertaining is, without a doubt, important. Some contacts (customers, suppliers and others) will not give their support and goodwill so readily if you appear to be taking it for granted. Yet time is finite and you cannot do this every time you think of it; each occasion should result from a considered decision and be worthwhile in its own right. Consider also simpler options. A meal out in a good restaurant or hotel may be too time consuming for your contact (they are in all probability busy people too) as well as yourself. What simpler options are there? For example, can something be arranged in the office? It must be done well, but it does not need to be a gigantic meal or a time consuming occasion to meet its objectives. You may well find this option is welcomed by some of your contacts.

Secondly, consider the phrase 'working lunch'. This is more often internal, and can be very simple – an urgent meeting scheduled for an hour one lunchtime with just coffee and sandwiches provided makes for productivity. Similarly, you may opt to go out for a simple snack with a colleague and do so to discuss a particular thing, often one that has escaped fitting into your schedule for too long. All this is useful. Sometimes lunchtime needs to be in the nature of a pause, but remember with around 220 working days in the year, and taking just an hour at each for lunch, adds up to more than 25 working days! So it is certainly an area to be thought about extremely carefully.

A final, cautionary, note: watch what you drink at lunchtime. Alcohol may help the atmosphere during lunch, but too much is not going to help you maintain or improve productivity in the afternoon. I wonder how often a secretary tells someone on the telephone 'He's not back from lunch', and means he is asleep at his desk?

Consider a day out

Entertaining was referred to in the previous section, but it can take many forms and some of them are a good deal more time consuming than lunch. Corporate entertaining (and I am not thinking so much of major group occasions such as sponsorship events) can include a wide variety of things from a night at the opera, to an evening in a karaoke bar; from a day at the races to an afternoon of golf. Because they involve a very real cost, such things certainly need thinking about, but so too do the time considerations.

Take a golf outing as an example. Much business really is, I am sure, conducted on the golf course and I am not suggesting that such activity is never useful and should be entirely rejected, but its real merits do need assessing. It is not enough that you will enjoy whatever it is, or that the contact will do so – what will come of it? Will it genuinely move the relationship forward? Is there another way of achieving the same effect with less time expenditure? Can anyone else do it? All these questions need answering. Other factors come in here too. A golf outing on a Saturday morning, rather than on a weekday, may be a good use of working time, though too many may begin to eat into family time. If three contacts accompany you on one day, then the time may be viewed differently from when there is only one.

Like so much discussed in this book, one more golf outing does not seem vasly significant, but it adds up. Two golf outings a month might use up the equivalent of a whole day, five per cent of your working time. You need to keep this in mind. Maybe a larger group of people once a month would work equally well. Whatever things of this nature form part of your working life, think about them not as an automatic part of the way things are, something that cannot be changed, but as time that needs to be utilised carefully just like any other. Then you can make the right decisions and know that time is not being wasted.

However and wherever contact occurs with other people, the nature of it will affect the duration of it. Being aware of this, especially in terms of the negative aspects of contact – and avoiding it – will save time.

No conflict – no wasted time

Now listen, pay attention. It is no good just sitting there lazily scanning the pages, you have to read this properly and . . . Not a good start. Sometimes an approach that is designed to get straight to the point and therefore not waste time has the reverse effect, it rubs people up the wrong way. This ends up producing misunderstanding, dissent or argument which in turn take time to resolve and the original intention goes out the window. Conflict is not, in fact, entirely bad. It can act as a catalyst to debate, it can help promote creativity and serve to drive for the results necessary in business. But there is a real difference between this and allowing unnecessary conflict to disrupt the smooth running of things and your time being affected along with it.

I am not suggesting here that the wrong decisions should be made for the sake of a quiet life, but in a number of areas conflict is to be avoided, for example:

- in communications: it may be necessary to persuade rather than cajole, and time taken to do so successfully may pay dividends
- office politics (of which there is always some) can become intrusive and time consuming; though ignoring it is dangerous in other ways, it must be kept in its place
- personalities can become more important than issues; commercial reason must dictate most of what directs an organisation, and untangling personality factors once they have got out of hand takes time
- sectional interests also have to be watched

Take this last as a simple example. Imagine that some internal reorganisation is to change the physical layout of an office, departments are going to move and, not surprisingly, sections are worried about the priority they will be given and the new conditions they will find. Yet there are entirely practical issues too. The design department needs good lighting, the customer services department needs the most telephones, a department with large amounts of stock in and out may need to be on the ground floor to take some very general ones. If consideration of what will be decided, any discussions, meetings and everything to do with the process can be kept primarily on a practical basis (there are other issues, of course); if conflict, in this case about personal issues, can be avoided, the time taken to sort the whole thing out will almost certainly be less. This has wide implications, but shows the merit of always bearing in mind the time element of everything with which you are concerned.

You may well say, with some justification, that some conflict can be advantageous. It can, on occasion, prompt creativity. This is quite different, however, to the kind of thing mentioned above which is an aggravation and waste of time without being useful. Circumstances which can create time wasting because of conflict can be momentary, something only demanding a moment's thought to avoid, or more intractable, demanding real effort and will power to avoid when you are itching to draw up battle lines. In either case, you should be on the look out for such circumstances and act to avoid their worst effects.

In addition, there may be more permanent prompts to such situations and these too need to be avoided. As an example, and something in any case worth a word of warning, consider the circumstances of dual reporting or, in other words, what happens if someone has, in effect, two bosses.

With the budgetary pressure on many organisations these days it is not uncommon for staffing levels to be under pressure too, and one symptom of this may be that organisation structure is made to accommodate multiple reporting relationships. This may be in seemingly simple areas, such as two executives sharing a secretary, or it may be more complex, as with a computer complex reporting in part to Finance and in part to Administration. Either way it is not ideal.

There are likely to be clashes in priorities. Unless there is a clear hierarchy with the two sharing a secretary, whose work gets done first? It may be fine most of the time, but when it causes problems it tends to cause awkward ones and the likelihood is something will end up being late. Our other example may pose much more radical clashes, maybe a proposed new programme to be used in the computer department suits one of its masters and not the other. Buying two versions might double an already significant cost. Who wins?

The one certainty with any situation of this sort is that sorting out the overlaps takes time, actual productivity is reduced and time is taken up on activity only made necessary by the way things are organised. Multi-boss reporting is not usually a good idea (there are no doubt exceptions); it affects the people involved, and may regularly put them in awkward positions between the two parties. It also affects other management issues: who appraises the person, sets their salary, acts as their overall supervisor? All are made more difficult. So, there are a number of good reasons to avoid this situation, and time management and achieving suitable productivity is a key one.

2 MANAGING OTHERS

Here a number of points are investigated predominantly for those who, as managers, have other people reporting to them. Many of the points made will have relevance to others on the receiving end of such a relationship, or whose job is likely to include such responsibilities at some time in the future.

The logical starting point is perhaps when such relationships are created. Finding the right person for any job is a vital and complex business (a management task often underestimated in my experience, leading to a systematic approach being neglected in light of the strong feeling that 'I can judge people'; it reminds one of how rarely you meet anyone who will admit to being a poor driver and seems to be an area where pride overcomes circumspection). There are many considerations, certainly too many for the brief of this book to explore comprehensively, but one certainly links to our theme.

Recruiting and selecting time efficient people

Successful management is dependent on many things and there is genuine difficulty in putting them in any sort of rank order. Successful recruitment and selection is, however, certainly one of the key ones and many other things are, in turn, dependent on it. Management is usually defined as achieving results *through* other people (rather than for them) and in a commercial organisation the objectives towards which you must work and the ultimate results are primarily economic. It is thus different from the things you do – your executive role – and you are dependent on how well your people perform for the overall results for which you are held responsible. If you recruit the wrong people, nothing else you can do may be able to make up for this, and results will suffer.

Given people of equal technical ability, then one factor that will condition their success, making it either better or worse, is their productivity; time management affects us all. Finding the right people is a skill. Most of us are not inherently able to look people over and form an instant and correct decision as to whether they will perform well or not, however much we might like to think we can. Curiously people are very myopic in this area, so selection must be a systematic process. It is rather like completing a jigsaw puzzle; gradually from the application form, interview, observations and references you put together a sufficient picture on which to make a judgement. It is never complete and you need to be aware that most people are putting on their very best face throughout this process. They are unlikely to turn out better than you think and may well be just a little less good.

In addition to the technical abilities you want, whether you are seeking someone who can type, sell or administer, there are other characteristics you will wisely bear in mind.

Some of the other points you want are subjective: will they fit in, will they outgrow the job too quickly? You will also want general characteristics that fit them to work in your office and one of these can perfectly well be having time management skills. They will display some – or should. Are they on time for the interview? Has any deadline for the receipt of applications been met? Is their application form well, legibly and completely filled in (avoiding time being wasted in checking)? You may want to ask them questions about how they organise themselves. I do not suggest this is easy, that there is any one magic question that will ascertain whether people are good in this way or not, and you may not be able to be certain when you make an appointment the candidate does have the right characteristics in this respect or not. But to ignore it is irresponsible and if you are, or succeed in becoming, a good manager of your time you will find it permanently frustrating to be surrounded by people who, whatever their other good characteristics, are a time utilisation nightmare.

With the people in place then you can consider what aspects of management are linked most closely to time management. One such is a key aspect of communication.

The need for clear instructions

There is an old saying that there is never time to do anything properly, but there must always be time to do it again. Nothing is more likely to end up meaning something has to be re-done than not making it clear to people what they had to do in the first place. It has already been said here that communication is not easy, but the responsibility for getting it right is with the communicator – and that, if you are issuing instructions, is you. Similarly, if people do not really understand and fail to query it, perhaps because they are worried you will blame them, then that is your fault also because you should make it clear that in such circumstances it is the way they should proceed.

So instructions should be clear and people should be told:

- *what* needs to be done (and give them sufficient details)
- *why* it needs to be done (knowing the objectives may make the task clearer and will improve the motivation)
- *how* it should be done (methodology etc.)
- *when* it should be completed (and anything else about the timing)

Before leaving the point, ask if it is clear – get some feedback. Any short cut of this sequence must be on the basis of genuine knowledge or familiarity, not simply assumption that all will be well. Good clear instructions save time, written guidelines do the same and for some jobs they are useful. This last is especially true of awkward or difficult jobs which are performed regularly but not often. One such job in my office is changing the toner unit on the laser printer. It is not *that* complicated, but frankly it is difficult to do after the time gap usually involved without reference to a chart of diagrams that came with the machine and which shows clearly the sequence of actions needed to complete the task. The moment taken to get this chart out is tiny, much less than even minor pause for puzzlement about how to make the change if it is not used, and it is all too easy with such a task to get in a real muddle and waste a considerable amount of time. Moral: all instructions, in whatever form, must be clear.

Don't do it – delegate

If a task simply has to be done, but you cannot get to it, then the best way to give yourself more time is to delegate the doing of it to someone else. This is eminently desirable and yet, for some, curiously difficult. First, consider the advantages, and do this by asking yourself what sort of manager you want to work for yourself. You could probably list a great many qualities: someone who is fair, who listens, who is decisive, good at their job and so on – but I would bet you put someone who delegates high on the list. The opposite is a boss who hangs on to everything, does not involve you, is probably secretive and generally not the sort of person you would want to work for at all. So if you delegate effectively, there are major advantages in other ways: motivation and the chance to tackle new things for one, as well as the time you will save.

Secondly, let us look at the difficulties. Delegating is a risk. Something may go wrong and what is more, as the manager, you may be blamed. So, despite the fact that going about it the right way will minimise the risk, there is temptation to hang on to things. This makes for problems in two ways. You have too much to do, and particularly too much at the more routine end, keeping you from giving the attention you know they deserve to things that are clear priorities. And staff do not like it, so motivation – and productivity on the things they are doing – will also be adversely affected.

But there is another important and significant reason why delegation sometimes does not happen. This is fear, not that the other person will not be able to cope, but that they will cope *too* well, that they will improve the method, that they will do things more quickly, more thoroughly and better in some way than you. If you are honest you may admit this is a real fear too; certainly it is as common as the fear that people will not cope. But it is not a reason that should put you off delegating – the potential rewards are too great. The amount you can do if you delegate successfully is way beyond the improvement in productivity you can hope to achieve *in any other way*. So it is a vital area. But what about something delegated that does go better? So much to the good, this is one of the key ways that progress is made in organisations as new people, new ways, and new thinking are brought to bear on tasks. Without it organisations would become stultified and unable to cope with change. And besides, as manager you should be the reason they are able to make this happen. It is your selection, development, counselling and management that creates and maintains a strong and effective team; and this is something for which you deserve credit.

All that is necessary to make delegation successful is a considered and systematic approach to the process. Such an approach is now reviewed. First let there be no doubt just how important this is. What does successful delegation achieve? There are five key results.

- it creates, for those to whom matters are delegated, opportunity for development and accelerated experience
- it builds morale (precisely because of the opportunity above) through the motivational effect of greater job satisfaction, and achievement long and short term in the job (and ultimately beyond it)
- it has broader motivational effects around a team, as well as on the individual

In addition, there are advantages to those who do the delegating, principally that as a result of the time freed up they can:

- concentrate time and effort on those aspects of their job which are key to the achievement of objectives
- bring a more considered, or creative, approach to bear, uncluttered by matters which may distract or prevent a broad brush or longer term perspective

You can probably think of specific advantages springing from these kinds of general effects in your own job. Yet it can be curiously difficult to delegate, and there are some managers who find it impossible. Because of this it is certainly worth asking the question what kind of person do you wish to report to? Most will answer: one who delegates – and so, no doubt, will those who work for you. If the time gains to be made from delegation seem inadequate to make you do it, or do it as much as you should, maybe this will produce additional pause for thought.

Despite the several and considerable advantages delegation can bring, it is not without its risks. It is this element of risk that can make it difficult to accomplish. But the risks can be minimised.

MINIMISING THE RISKS

There is always the possibility that delegation will not work. After all, it passes on 'the right to be wrong' as it were, by putting someone else in the driving seat. So if a misjudgement is made about the choice of what is to be delegated, to whom it is to be delegated or how the process will be carried out, things may end up with mistakes being made, and time being wasted as a result. In fact, while the possibility of failure is a classic reason why delegation is not instigated, there is another equally powerful motivation. This can exert as much, if not more, pressure for no action to be taken; that is the fear that something will be delegated and far from not going well *it will be done even better than the delegators can do it themselves*. This is worth a little honest thought. How many managers can really put their hand on their heart and say that they have never resisted delegating for this reason? Yet this is precisely how an organisation may change and grow, by bringing different minds to bear on the tasks to be undertaken and evolving better and better ways of doing things. In fact, therefore, delegation that leads to creative change is all credit to those who make it happen – on both sides of the delegation process. Although if things go wrong the delegators must shoulder the blame, as they retain the ultimate responsibility, in any case the objective should be to maximise the utilisation of your time through delegation, and gain the other advantages around the team.

The net intention from all this must be to minimise the inherent risks, first by selecting tasks that are suitable for delegation. In most jobs there will be certain things that should sensibly be omitted. These include:

- matters key to overall results generation or control
- staff discipline matters
- certain contentious issues (e.g. staff grievances)
- confidential matters (though be sure they need to be confidential, protecting unnecessary secrets can be very time wasting and often fruitless)

Then, in picking the best person to whom to delegate, you should ask questions such as:

- have they undertaken similar tasks in the past?
- do they have the necessary knowledge, experience and capability?
- is it too much to cope with at once?
- is prior training (however informal) necessary?
- do they *want* to do more? (or should they?)
- will they be acceptable to others involved and will it be accepted also as a fair opportunity amongst peers?

Thereafter, perhaps the greatest guarantee of success is clear communication, and that does not just mean with the person involved, but more widely as necessary. Others may have to know what is going on and have to trust in the person's ability to do something. Messages may need to be passed up and down and across the line to ensure total clarity. Make sure there is nothing left out regarding authority, responsibility and that, above all, the individual concerned knows why the job is necessary and why they are doing it. And be confident as the result of any briefing that they are able to do it satisfactorily.

Any explanation needs to make clear whether what is being done is a one-off exercise, perhaps in an emergency situation, or ultimately a permanent addition to the existing set of responsibilities. Remember delegation is more than simple work allocation and, as such, has implications for such matters as job descriptions and even salary and employment conditions.

Assuming that delegation is well chosen and communicated, the next step is to keep in touch, at least initially, with how things are going.

MONITORING PROGRESS

Once something has been passed over, keeping in touch can easily be forgotten, and when done can present certain problems. It must be done, in a word, *carefully*. If it is not then it will smack of interference and may doom the whole process. The simplest way to monitor in an acceptable way is to build in any necessary checks at the time of the original briefing and handover. From the beginning, ask for interim reports at logical points. Do not simply arrive unannounced at someone's desk and ask to see the file (they may be at an awkward stage). Let them bring things to you, and to an agreed deadline. If they have been well briefed, know what is expected and to what standards, then they can deliver in a way that either duplicates past practice, or brings something new to the activity. Either may be appropriate in the short term, though, as nothing lasts for ever, new thinking is usually to be encouraged once the person has a real handle on the basics.

It may be necessary to let things proceed, to bite your tongue and resist taking the whole matter back during this stage as you see things proceeding in a way that may well differ, if only a little, from the way in which you would have done the job. The ultimate results make all this worthwhile, and not just in time terms but in terms of growth and development within the workplace.

So far so good. If all goes well surely there is nothng more to be done? Wrong. The process must be evaluated.

EVALUATING HOW DELEGATION HAS WORKED

Once sufficient time has gone by and you can assess how things have gone, a number of questions should be asked. These can usefully include:

- has the task been completed satisfactorily?
- did it take an acceptable amount of time?
- does it indicate the person concerned could do more?
- are there other tasks that could be delegated along the same route?
- what has been the effect on others? (e.g. are others wanting more responsibility?)
- is there any documentation change necessary as a result?
- has any new or revised methodology been created and are there

implications arising from this (e.g. a change to standing instructions)?

and overall what has the effect on productivity been?

This last brings us to a key aspect of evaluation: what has the effect been on *you*? In other words:

- what have you done with the time saved? (this might make new work possible, or facilitate a greater focus on key or long term issues).

There is little to be gained by delegating if you only end up submerged in more detail and having little or nothing of real substance to show for the change.

Similarly, should the process not be a success, questions should be asked about what went wrong and they too need to address both sides, asking not just what did someone else do wrong or misunderstand, but also raising such questions as how thoroughly you in fact briefed that person. It is important to learn from the experience; testing what you delegate, to whom and seeking the best way of handling the process is well worthwhile. If you develop good habits in this area it can pay dividends over time.

At the end of the day the effect on others is as important as the effect on you. People carry out with the greatest enthusiasm and care those things for which they have responsibility. In delegating you pass on the opportunity for additional responsibility (strictly speaking responsibility can only be taken, you cannot force it on people) and you must also pass on with it the authority to act. As has been said, delegation fosters a good working relationship around a team of people. Not least it produces challenge and, although there are risks, people will normally strive hard to make it work and the failure rate will thus be low. Certainly the effect on productivity can be marked. But – there is always a but with anything of this sort – it is a process that needs care, determination and perhaps even sacrifice. Delegation is not just a way of getting rid of the things you regard as chores, amongst the matters most likely to benefit from delegation are almost certainly things you enjoy doing.

The potential rewards cannot be overrated, and the need to make delegation work is therefore strong. Theodore Roosevelt once said: 'The best executive is the one who has sense enough to pick good men to do what he wants done, and the self-restraint enough to keep from meddling with them while they do it'. Sound advice, and for the manager wanting to be a good time manager it is crucial. The two things go together. You cannot be as good at time management if you are a poor delegator. Get both right and you have a major part of the overall management process working for you.

This is an area to think on. Do you delegate? Do you delegate the right things and do it sufficiently often? How well does it work? While the principles reviewed here are important and it is something to be tackled on the right basis, an intention and commitment to making it work are perhaps even more important. It may be worth more time to check it out. If you think there is more that you could delegate, review just what and just how you can action the process to get the very most from it in terms of your time and all the other advantages that can flow from it. Perhaps you should consider attending a course on delegating (– or better still, send your assistant!)

Swap tasks to save time

Everyone has different skills and also different things they get done most quickly and easily. Some of the things you find laborious, a colleague may think a small matter. As everyone is in this position all you need to do is organise some exchanges. For example, in the sales office of one company where I did some work, two people did this very effectively. The department had to analyse, document and circulate sales results in various forms (to show sales progress, salesmen's targets and results by territory etc.). One person was very good at the analysis, sorting the untidy returns that came in from the sales team into an ordered set of information. Another was good at presenting the information in graphic form – something that would now be done, much quicker, by computer I expect.

In the official work allocation they had both been given the complete job to do for different product sales results. In effect they swapped and all the analysis was done by one, while all the graphic representation was done by the other. The entire job was completed more easily and faster and there was more time to apply to the other tasks, primarily dealing with customers, that made up their responsibilities. They felt it was a fair swap in time terms and all worked well.

This is something that can be done in all sorts of ways around groups of people working together, or even in different departments. There is only one snag to watch out for and that is any developmental role that is part of a job having been allocated to someone in the first place. If a manager expects you to become familiar with a task and build up some sort of expertise in it, then you are not likely to do that by letting someone else do the work. That apart, it works well as an idea and you may want to be on the look out for suitable swap situations that will help you. They must turn out to be fairly balanced, of course – if one party ends up with far more work than the other, then the arrangement will not last, as someone will end up unhappy. More complex swaps, for example, two smaller tasks for one larger one, may achieve a suitable balance. Choose well and you may evolve a number of such arrangements all around the organisation, each of which save you time. As long as the network does not become too complicated (it must continue to work when you are away for a while, and deadlines must be compatible) then it is one more useful way of saving time on a regular basis.

Develop your people

It was clear, I hope, in the previous paragraph that delegation is one of the greatest opportunities for the manager to create more time for himself. There is one potential snag, however. This is simply that the people to whom you delegate must have the necessary skill and aptitude to take on delegated tasks and make a good job of them. What their skill level actually is depends largely on you. You recruit and select them, and one of your responsibilities is helping them to develop.

Training and development is one of those things that most people agree is a 'good thing', yet it is also something that is all too easy to miss out when you are busy. Here is an additional reason to make sure that it does not get overlooked: help your people develop and they will help you do your job, because not only will the team perform better, but you will be able to delegate more to them.

As a responsible manager you should have an individual development plan for every single person who reports to you. This will stem in part from their annual appraisal meeting and evaluation, and can usefully include things that you will do, for example by personal counselling, things they will do, such as private study and experiment and practice, and things that, as it were, the organisation will do for them, such as sending them on a course or providing other training resources for them to use. The criteria that decide what development is necessary will arise from an analysis of a person's job, defining what is necessary to do it, then determining whether the person matches up to this or whether there is a skills gap that must be closed by training. In addition, the manager has to look ahead, asking how the job will be different in future because such changes may widen the training gap. Some things of this nature may be technological, such as when an operation is being computerised and the staff are going to need to understand how to use the new system. But they should also include a link with your job as manager and anticipate possible delegation opportunities. What tasks must you cope with during the next year and what other things might you shed to make room for the new things you have to tackle? The obvious choices for things to delegate are those that staff can already do competently. But it may well be worth looking more broadly at what possibilities there are if some development is done first?

This can be a classic case of a positive balance: time invested is necessary, but the payoff can often be well worthwhile. It is a pity if the longer term nature of this process makes it less likely to be taken advantage of because, not only will you save time, but it will also lead to the other advantages of delegation: personal motivation and stimulation to the process of running the organisation.

Simply the most time saving phrase in the language

There is a scene that is played out in offices all over the world and which must waste untold hours every single day. Imagine a manager is busy in his office when a head comes round the door and one of his staff comes in. 'What is it?' he asks. And the reply is something like: 'I am not sure how to handle so and so and wondered if you would just check it with me'. The manager thinks for a second. He is busy – in the middle of a job and not wanting to lose concentration – but he has already been interrupted. So his first thought is to minimise the interruption so he can get back to work fast. So, if the matter allows, he spends a minute or two explaining what to do and then tells the other person to let him get on and the brief impromptu meeting is over. This may be done kindly or abruptly, the effect is much the same, and the scene may be played out many times in a day by the one manager.

But suppose the same manager is away from the office for a couple of days. While he is away the same member of his staff will face similar situations. If the manager was in his office they would go and ask. Because he is not, they simply get on with the job, they make a decision, they take action, and life goes on. When the manager returns to the office what does he find? A chain of diasters? A plethora of wrong decisions and misjudged actions? Rarely is this the case. The things that would have been checked if he had been there have been actioned, and not only is no harm done, everything has probably gone perfectly well.

Think about it. I suspect this picture will ring bells with many, if not most, managers. Why does it happen? It is a classic case of thinking that it is quicker to do things for people, most often in this case providing the answer or the decision, rather than to take any other action. I believe this is wrong. You have to take a longer term view, and this is where the most time saving phrase in the language comes in.

Next time you are interrupted in the way I have described, try responding by saying: 'What do *you* think you should do?' They may not know, but you can press the point, prompt them to make some suggestions, and when they do, then ask which solution they think is best. This takes a few minutes, certainly longer than the earlier response, but if they are coping when you are not there to ask, then you will find that when you prompt them they most often come up with a good answer (in business there is rarely any one *right* way). At that point you can say something like: 'that's fine', and away they go to carry on, leaving you to get back to your own work.

Now this is not just a better way of dealing with this situation – indeed at this stage you may say it is worse as it prolongs the interruption. It is doing something else of very real value; it is teaching them not to interrupt, but rather to have the confidence to think it through for themselves. You have to be insistent about this. It will not work if you only make them think it through when you have more time, and still provide a quick answer when you are busy. Every time – every single time – someone comes through the door with a question about something with which you believe they should be able to deal unaided, you say: 'What do you think you should do?' It must become a catch phrase. And as this practice continues the message will get home to them, so that if they even start to think of asking you they can hear your likely response in their mind. If you do this you will find such questions coming less and less often. You will find that if they do ask, they move straight to the second stage, and come in with two or three thought out options just wanting you to say which is best. Resist; ask them. The message will stick and, surprise, surprise, you will find you are saving time. What is more, your people will almost certainly get to like it more also, especially if you comment favourably on how well they are doing on the decisions they are making unaided.

This is one of the best tested and useful time savers there is – the most time saving phrase in the language – and all it needs is some persistence and determination. Early on you may think it is taking too much time, but the investment formula will surely pay off. There are considerable amounts of time to be saved here, linked in fact to the number of people who report to you. Do not be faint hearted about this, it is very easy to break your resolve in a busy moment and send someone on their way with an instant dictated solution. Exceptions to your consistency will just make the lesson take longer to get over. But this idea really does work in the longer term; not to operate this way does your people a disservice and allows you to miss out on one of the best time savers managers can find.

The short encounter described here might qualify as a meeting, but before considering meetings, which are very important to good time management, there are a number of more general points to bear in mind.

Do not hover

However work has been passed on, whether it is simple work allocation or a job that has been delegated, managers have to give members of their team space to complete the tasks they are working on. There is a temptation, perhaps particularly when a job is first delegated and you worry whether it will be done right, not only to check up but to do so on an *ad hoc* basis. Because this is off-putting to those who may be at some mid-point on a job – a point at which things are not finished and look that way – it can actually end up delaying things and perhaps give you a false impression of their capabilities. These checks take time and may set back the way things are going rather than help. Certainly they do nothing for motivation.

Do not hover. If something needs checking, and it may well do, then such checks should be discussed and agreed at the start of the work. Then the people concerned know what to expect. They can plan for any checks at particular moments and such checks will, as a result, be more likely to be constructive – or indeed unnecessary as those concerned will work to make sure that when the monitoring process arrives all will be on schedule.

If you work to make such checks an agreed part of the plan, if you make them constructive, then you will not have to spend very much time on them at all. The team working well, with minimal supervision, is a great asset to any manager wanting to conserve their own time.

Motivate your people

Motivation is a powerful force. As Fig. 7.1 shows, by acting on their knowledge and ability it can improve performance, efficiency and productivity – and save time. But, like so much else in management, this does not just happen. Unless you work at it, and that means some time will be taken up, you will not get the best from people, and that means some time will be wasted. Again the equation of time here makes sense; the net effect should be a saving.

PERFORMANCE = (KNOWLEDGE + ABILITY) x MOTIVATION

Fig. 7.1 The motivation formula

Motivation has been described as a climate and this is not a bad analogy. Just like the climate or the temperature in a room, it is affected by many different things, and the effect can be for good or ill. There is sadly no magic formula for guaranteeing that motivation will be, and will stay, high. You have to look at the motivational implications of things such as the administration and systems with which people work, the way they relate to colleagues and you as supervisor, their feeling of security in the sense of knowing what they have to do and being part of a good team. All these can pull motivation down if they are organised badly or unsympathetically.

Similarly, there are many influences that boost people's motivation such as the enjoyment of the work and, more particularly, a sense of satisfaction and achievement in doing it and doing it well. All these and more are important (and it is a subject worth some study if you manage others). One factor, which makes a useful example of how the small things matter, concerns the recognition of achievement. People do not just like to achieve, they like recognition of that to be shown. Some of this may come in tangible form – bonuses, incentives, commission on sales, prize schemes etc. – but some of it is much simpler.

For example, most people who are busy cannot, in all honesty, put their hands on their hearts and say that they always remember the little things as much as they should. Think about it yourself. Have you said 'thank you' or 'well done' often enough lately? It matters, people notice and they expect it. More than that, there are moments when a lunch, or a drink at the end of the day are deserved and appreciated. It takes only a few moments, but it keeps the team operating together and such time can be handsomely repaid in the future in the form of smoother, more self-contained, working.

All such rewards, large or small (and a 'thank you' costs nothing) must be earned. I am not suggesting that you go round spraying out platitudes without cause. The cause/effect relationship is important, and needs to be visible. Provided there is good work being done then this kind of activity can maintain and develop the attitudes that foster it. Remember motivation is essentially long term. It takes time to change attitudes and you should not expect instant results; more you should see all these inputs as creating over time a productive team which will then work effectively in all the ways that make your time go further.

Provide specific time management help to staff

People who work together in an office can be infected by the prevailing practices and habits. In an office where some people habitually arrive late in the morning and nothing is said, more people will tend to follow suit and the situation will spread and get worse. This is a negative point, but here I am more concerned with the positive. If you want time management to be an issue that people care about, think about and work at, then you must take the initiative and lead by example.

Several practices may be useful here, for example:

- *set up standard systems*: it is not too dictatorial to set up, and insist on, certain systems that you feel will help everyone's time utilisation, for example, the same priority codes used around the office, the same basis for completing diaries (or even the same diary or time system), an insistence on tidy desks – you can probably think of more.
- *use standard reporting procedures*: here again a standard helps; such things as memo style, when, where and how meetings are scheduled, notice boards, all can help create a climate of efficiency if they are well organised
- *explain*: if you tell people why you do certain things, work in certain ways and why you expect them to do likewise then it is more likely that, seeing a good and personally useful reason, they will comply (you can go further and organise training for them)

Once practice in these things occurs, habits follow and then the time saving around and amongst a group of people accumulates. So be a public advocate for the virtues of time management, say you believe in it, say you practise it, and do not just expect your team to follow suit – make it easy for them by introducing them to the systems and laying down a few rules to make it all stick. If you help them in these kinds of ways, it will help you too.

Make and keep some firm rules

The days of dictatorial management have, by and large, long gone. Management in today's environment necessarily involves consultation. It makes sense. People will go along much more whole-heartedly with things – policies, practices, whatever – if they feel they have played some part in their origination. At its most powerful this creates what is nowadays called ownership and is a force for commitment and getting results. But there are limits. Just because consultation is a good thing, it does not mean that you have to consult, interminably, over everything. To balance the time this takes you need other areas where, while the policy is sensibly constituted, there is no debate and no time wasted on it.

An example will perhaps help make this clear. Every office has administration and form filling that needs to be done. It seems a chore but the information is no doubt useful in some way or should be! (Why else is it being completed?). Sometimes in an office this form filling is resisted. People know it is useful, but they also see other things as more important. They probably are, but that does not mean that the forms should never get filled in, besides the individual contributions may, when collated together, provide key information. So, what happens? People delay, forms come in late or incomplete and have to be returned and redone, sometimes more than once.

In one office I know this was the case with the kind of control forms which field salesmen must complete to keep sales figures and the customer database updated. Salesmen are notoriously bad at administration and the forms would regularly appear late, maybe half – and a different half – needing chasing each month. The sales manager's secretary wasted time doing the chasing, and the sales manager had to keep explaining to his boss why the collated statistics were not available, as even one outstanding meant that the collation could not take place. It was generally messy and unsatisfactory and something had to be done to sharpen things up.

The sales manager thought about it. First he checked that the system was the minimum necessary, and that the forms were straightforward to complete. He thought of various checks, but reckoned each could well waste still more time. Finally, he hit on the following scheme: he revised the instruction about the system so that no one was to be reimbursed their monthly expenses until all their forms were received and were passed as clear, legible and complete. Eureka! Overnight the behaviour was changed and the forms all arrived on time. What is more the effect lasted and I now know a number of companies who use the exact same incentive. The salesmen in fact saw this as reasonable, they knew the system was necessary, the new announcement was well put and the results spoke for themselves.

The most important thing happening here was that there was a group agreement that certain things simply had to go right without a lot of time being spent to achieve them. The incentive is neat and makes it a nice example, but there might be numbers of things a manager could do in such circumstances to add a bit of an edge to the rule. The important thing is that there should be certain areas where you operate in this sort of way. There is a firm rule, possibly a sanction, and it is clearly understood that there will be no exceptions, no excuses and no time wasted. If something does go wrong having set things up on this basis, then you have to descend from a great height and read the riot act – and do so consistently.

There is another major time saver. Have a think about the things that go on in your office and amongst your people. You may well have some candidate systems or procedures that are due this sort of treatment. If so, start working on them soon. It is additionally another area that not only can, of itself, save time, but which helps to position attitudes and develop the right habits.

130 Let them take a seat

As a not entirely serious note on which to end this section, here is an idea that seems to work, though it is not for everyone. Early in my career I worked with someone who was an excellent time manager. He used many of the systems and taught me many of the ideas now incorporated into this book. His work involved seeing a great many people from outside the organisation. Not all of these meetings were useful, and some turned out to be a waste of time. Not only that, but experience had taught him to be a pretty accurate judge in advance of which were going to waste time.

To combat this he had one of the chairs in his office adapted. The front legs were made just one inch shorter than the back. Now this is not dramatic and it does not show (at least it withstood a normal glance – perhaps people did notice but did not believe it), but it *is* curiously less comfortable than usual. He always swore that he could measure the amount of time saved as people excused themselves earlier than might otherwise have been the case. I was never quite sure about this – but I wonder? Try it, it certainly is just a bit uncomfortable. Maybe it is worth a try, if only for your staff!

Certainly you should not necessarily maximise comfort for every visitor. If they are sitting in an easy chair, drinking the second cup of coffee you insisted on – 'Go on, just one more cup' – then the circumstances dictate something about the remaining duration of the meeting. You cannot say 'Goodbye' just as they add the sugar to a full cup. This is the sort of thing where time wasted can add up over the course of the year. Do not, of course, be unsuitably inhospitable, but think a moment before you overdo it as it could take more time than you want or is warranted for either party.

3 MEETINGS
(and how to survive them)

It is said that the ideal meeting is one of two people – with one absent! And another saying (and the title of a training film) refers to Meetings, Bloody Meetings. There is truth in both comments, yet meetings are an important part of organisational communication, consultation and debate. We need them. Or certainly we need some of them, but we must get the most from them, and we do not need too many, or those that are longer than necessary nor, above all, those that are unconstructive. So, this is an important topic to relate to time management. It may represent a substantial amount of time on your time log, and thus be an area of potential time saving of some significance. Some of the points here may seem simple, but they may be deceptive in that they demand discipline and they can each save considerable time.

The first thing to consider about meetings is absurdly simple:

Is your meeting (really) necessary?

How often have you come out of a meeting and not only been dissatisfied but wondered what you were doing there or even why the meeting was held at all? If you answer never, then you must work for an extraordinary organisation, and if it is often you are in good company. There are two situations we must consider here: your meetings and others to which you are invited.

YOUR MEETINGS

Before you open your mouth to say, 'let's set a meeting', pause, think – and think of the alternatives. Ask questions: is it a matter for debate or consultation, or can you make a decision without that? Can any information that will be disseminated at the meeting be circulated any other way? If brief conversation is necessary, is it enough to have a word on the telephone, in the corridor or over a working lunch? Often the answer presents an alternative, and a briefer one than a meeting. If so, make a telephone call, send a note or take whatever action may be called for to achieve what you want.

Remember here that you are not just talking about your time, but that of everyone at the meeting. Six people meeting for an hour represents the equivalent of six hours' work, and this is the right way to think of it. Indeed bear in mind that it is more than six hours' work as people have to prepare, to get there (in some situations this is a significant amount of time) and others such as secretaries may be involved in setting up the occasion and seeing to the arrangements. It is an important part of any meeting convener's responsibility to think carefully about who those six, or however many, people should be, remembering that every time another name is added to the list, not only will this take up that person's time but the meeting itself will take longer for everyone than it would with fewer participants.

OTHERS' MEETINGS

With these, while there will be some you must attend, the same applies: think first before you agree to participate. You may find there are things you attend for the wrong reasons, for example, it is very easy to find you are going just to keep in touch, or just in case something important crops up. Maybe the minutes are sufficient to accommodate this. Or maybe, if you are a manager, it is important for your section to be represented, but you can delegate someone else to attend and report back to you afterwards. This may take some resolve. There may be aspects of the meeting you enjoy, topics on which your contribution allows you to shine, but it may still not be a priority to attend. There is an old story, which perhaps shows the attitude to take, about a Training Manager who scheduled a management course on delegating skills and sent round a note indicating that certain managers were expected to attend. One replied promptly saying he would not attend, but would send his assistant! But I digress.

In either case, whatever the meeting is about, make sure it is essential, that there is no alternative and if it has to be, then read the rest of this section before you finalise matters and the meeting gets under way. If you have to have it you will want to make sure it is productive.

Do not perpetuate regular meetings

This is a perennial issue in many organisations. There are monthly, weekly, even daily meetings that occur on that particular frequency for no better reason than that they have become a habit. This can lead so easily to time being wasted that I am not even in favour of anything having the name 'monthly so and so meeting'; it makes it just too easy to keep them going. Sometimes, of course, these are necessary, but on other occasions there is nothing, or nothing very much, to discuss and the meeting may then be padded out to make it worthwhile (it can, in fact, do the opposite).

So if a meeting is to be held a number of times through the year, consider not just the frequency, but specifically the number and placement of such meetings. For example, maybe you do not need 12 monthly meetings, but ten and at some times of the year you need them closer together, at others (for example holiday times) you can have longer gaps between them. This kind of scheduling will almost always save time.

It is also good practice to schedule meetings well ahead. So for the situation referred to above you would set ten dates for the year ahead, adding a new tenth every time you met to keep the future arrangement the same. Everyone knows the problem of getting a group of busy people together at short notice, so this will always work much better, particularly if the people involved are disciplined about their diaries and do not allow themselves to be double booked. Certain meetings are clearly priority occasions and should be kept firm, remembering that any change disrupts a number of people and thus wastes a disproportionate amount of time.

In this way meetings will be perceived as reflecting their role, rather than any mechanistic formula of, for example, 'once a month.'

Cancel meetings

This is a brief point, and links to the topic of regular meetings covered in the last paragraph, but there is an issue here that can waste large amounts of time so it deserves a mention in its own right. It is surprising and curious how meetings that are scheduled for a good reason still run even when the good reason has not only gone but everyone knows it has gone. It is difficult to understand. Perhaps someone thinks it is too late to cancel (I would rather hear two minutes before the meeting that it is cancelled than turn up and waste time), or they think that it will still be useful as minor matters can be dealt with 'as the people are coming together'. Usually such thinking is wrong. It is better to cancel, or postpone if the main reason has not gone away forever.

This is especially true of regular series of meetings. The example of ten meetings being held through a year is the kind of thing where it is often better to schedule ten knowing you are in fact likely only to need eight or nine. The disruption of one dropped is very much less than pulling an extra one together at short notice, and this should become the habit. Never go ahead just because it is 'the regular meeting' or you will waste time.

Always have a specific reason for meeting

Obvious perhaps, but meetings are held every day without real – or clear – objectives, and take longer and become muddled as a result. And having objectives does *not* mean meeting to:

- start the planning process
- discuss cost savings
- review training needs
- streamline administration

or even to explore time saving measures.

Objectives should be specific. So to discuss how we might save ten per cent on the advertising budget over the next six months is better. Better still if that is a figure picked as achievable and it is something currently necessary (despite the effects it might have). At the end of the meeting we should be able to see if what the meeting was convened to achieve has really happened, or is likely to, for such an objective might take more than one short meeting to finalise.

So specific a statement – which should be in writing in many cases and circulated to all those due to participate – will have a number of effects:

- people will be clear why the meeting is being held
- they will be better able, and perhaps more inclined, to prepare
- discussion will be easier to control as people will focus more on the topic and the meeting will be more likely to achieve the desired result and to do so in less time than would be the case with a vague description

If you ever go to meetings where the objectives do not seem to be clear, ask what they are. Others may well agree that they are not clear and a few minutes spent early in the meeting clarifying this may be time well spent rather than launching into the discussion and finding that the meeting grinds to a halt in confusion half an hour later. Better still, ask before you attend. A clear objective is a real necessity; no meeting without this is likely to conclude its business either promptly or satisfactorily.

Prepare a clear agenda

The word agenda, which comes from Latin, means literally 'those things which must be done', and a key thing that must be done is drawing up a written agenda and, for many meetings, circulating it in advance. Again this is basic, but it is often omitted and can be the cause of confusion and thus waste of time. The agenda does not need to be elaborate but you should *always* have one. The agenda should do a number of things:

- specify the formalities (do you need to note apologies for absence, for example)
- pick up and link points from any previous meetings to ensure continuity
- give people an opportunity (as it is assembled) to input to the meeting content, if this is required
- specify who will lead or contribute in any particular way to each item, in part to facilitate preparation
- order the items for discussion or review; this is something that may need to represent the logical order of the topics, the difficulty they pose (and perhaps the time they will take), the participants' convenience (maybe someone has to leave early and you want something to be dealt with early on while they are still present)

- reflect any 'hidden' agenda; for example, with a controversial issue being placed to minimise discussion (perhaps just before lunch)
- deal with administrative matters such as where and when the meeting will be held, and, if it is long, whether appropriate refreshments will be served

You should check the overall look and balance of the agenda to make sure that too much is not being attempted in the time. If patience runs out things will end up taking longer or will not have justice done to them. And, perhaps above all, the agenda should reflect the objectives set for the meeting, indeed although a conventional agenda entry does not usually state why something is being discussed, you may find a longer version useful and that it actually acts to speed up the meeting.

Get the timing right

This whole book and the art of time management itself is built round the fact that time is a resource like any other, one worth conserving and utilising carefully. Here in the timing element of meetings is a chance to put this directly into practice. Basics first – every meeting needs a starting time. But when that is exactly can effect how productive the meeting will be. Set a time too late in the day and everyone is tired and enthusiasm may well be low; but it will be easier to stop it running on too long. Similarly, if you need a couple of hours for something then starting at 11.00 am will give you a couple of hours before lunch and again people will be less inclined to encourage the meeting to run on and on.

Perhaps an early start suits. At 8.00 or 8.30 am you may have a quiet hour before the switchboard opens and more interruptions are likely. It depends on the work pattern of your business and your office, but there are options here which make a difference. Once you are under way, there are other timing factors to worry about for example:

- *Finishing time:* every meeting should have not only a start time, but also a finish time. It is a courtesy to people, and helps keep the meeting on track, to set aside a specific amount of time for a session. You can always finish early, and should try hard not to overrun. If you always do this you will get better at and better judging how long things need.

- *A timed agenda:* similarly, it helps to have items on the agenda timed (perhaps not every last one, but certainly main headings and topics). Again this helps focus discussion and will give you something to aim for – 'let's try to get this out of the way in the next 20 minutes'. It really helps.

- *Respect for time:* this is especially important and starts right at the beginning. One of the greatest time wasters is the situation where some people, or even one person, is late for a meeting. You probably know the scenario only too well. People congregate, the time arrives for which the meeting is set, not everyone is present, it is decided to 'give them five minutes', coffee is poured, various *ad hoc* (and probably not very useful) discussions start amongst different groups, time passes and finally the meeting starts 15 minutes late with one person still to arrive. Ten minutes later, just as things are really getting down to business, the latecomer arrives. Apologies and recapping waste another five minutes. If there are, say, eight people at the meeting this scenario can waste as much as eight x half an hour, that is four hours – without, in some organisations, this even seeming exceptional. Imagine the waste in a large department or organisation over a year! The moral deserves emphasis:

ALWAYS START THE MEETING RIGHT ON TIME

Doing this may be awkward to start with, but the only way to crack this problem is to instil habits and respect. If you are new to a company or department, it is very much an area with which to start as you mean to go on. If someone is late, say so. Try not to recap (do it one to one if necessary at the end of the meeting – this will make more of a point). Be consistent, let the word go round: 'You'd better not be late for Patrick's meetings'. It really is worth the effort. It will probably never work perfectly, human nature being what it is, but you must either make a real effort to get close or admit defeat in an area where significant amounts of time will then continue to be wasted. There is also the danger that lack of discipline here will affect other areas. It is a good thing on which to make a stand, after all the problem gets compounded – if people know that meetings never start on time, they will not even aim for the starting time and things will be inclined to go from bad to worse.

Some people swear by one little trick here, they always schedule their meetings for an odd time. They are never at 9.00 am, or

3.30 pm; they are at 9.20 and 10.40. It makes a point, maybe it will help create order.

The things mentioned here are all important not only of themselves, but as visible signs of your attitude in this area as a potential instiller of good habits. One final word almost goes without saying – it is all helped immeasurably if you are punctual for any meeting you attend, and especially those you have convened!

Ensure a meeting is well chaired

Every meeting needs a chairman, or what is becoming known in these days of precision about lack of sexual bias, as 'the Chair'. More than that, every meeting needs a good chair, someone who can lead the meeting, handle the discussion, and generally act to see the objectives of the meeting are met and the agenda covered in the time allocated. It may be difficult to either take over or instruct a senior colleague in the art – and it is an art – of how to chair a session, but you can at least make sure that any meeting you are to run youself will be well chaired.

The benefits are then considerable:

- the meeting will better focused on its objectives
- discussion can be kept more constructive
- a thorough review can be assured before decisions are made
- all sides of an argument can be reflected, and balanced
- the meeting will be kept more businesslike and less argumentative (even in reviewing contentious issues)

and, above all, it will be more likely to run to time and achieve the results wanted promptly, efficiently and without waste of time.

The chairing of a meeting is a skill that must be learned and practised. It is worth some study. The checklist in Fig. 7.2 will remind you of the essentials, all of which can potentially save time if properly executed.

Whoever is chairing a meeting must:

- command the respect of those attending
- do their homework and come prepared, having read any relevant documents and taken any other necessary action to put themselves in a position to 'take charge' (it helps also if they encourage others to prepare, this makes for more considered and succinct contributions to the meeting and this saves time)
- be punctual
- start on time
- ensure administrative matters will be taken care of correctly (e.g. refreshments, someone to take the minutes etc.)
- start on the right note and lead into the agenda
- introduce the people, if necessary (and certainly know who's who – namecards can help at some kinds of meeting)
- set the rules – you surely need two, maybe more: only one person can talk at one time; the chair decides who
- control the discussion, and the individual types present (the talkative, the quiet, the argumentative etc.) encouraging contributions where necessary and asking questions to clarify (this last can be a great time saver – always query something unclear at once; it may take much longer to sort out if the meeting runs on with something being misinterpreted as it then becomes necessary to recap and recover a section)
- ensure everybody has their say
- keep the discussion to the point
- listen, as in LISTEN, so as to be able to resolve any 'But you said . . .' arguments
- watch the clock, and remind people of the time pressure
- summarise, clearly and succinctly, where necessary, which usually means regularly
- ensure decisions are actually made, agreed and recorded as necessary
- cope with upsets, outburst and emotion
- provide the final word (summary) and bring things to a conclusion (and link to any final administrative detail, things like setting another meeting date are often forgotten)
- see afterwards to any follow up action (another great time waster is people arriving at meetings having not taken action promised at a previous session)

and do all this with patience, goodwill, humour, and respect for the various individuals present.

Fig. 7.2 The essentials of chairing a meeting

Fig. 7.2, and certain others of the thoughts expressed over the last few pages, are drawn from work I did for my book *The Meetings Pocketbook* (Management Pocketbooks)

Never compete with interruptions

Even with some planning to prevent it, there are a variety of distractions that can and do take place during the course of meetings. Prevention is clearly best, but you may have to deal (and so does the Chair) with everything from tea and coffee being noisily delivered, to people being handed or leaving to collect or deal with messages – 'Sorry, but I just *must* attend to this one' – and the ubiquitous mobile telephone.

In all cases the best rule is usually to first acknowledge the distraction, then to wait till it has passed. Take a natural break while the tea and coffee are poured, for instance. A two minute 'stretch' break every now and then will help keep people alert in a long meeting, and prevent individuals causing a disturbance as they *have to* excuse themselves for a moment.

If interruptions are managed well, then time wasted will be kept to the minimum and key elements of the meeting – a presentation of some important plan, perhaps – will not lose effectiveness and impact by being only half heard or understood. This last only means more recapping and explanation which extends the time still more.

A good chairperson will think of such things in advance, time the refreshments to coincide with a natural break (and, ideally, the conclusion of an item on the agenda), make sure that mobile telephones and bleeping reminder systems are switched off, and that suitable instructions have been left with secretaries and switchboard operators about messages.

Consider carefully where to hold the meeting

The environment does make a difference to how a meeting succeeds, and if you are arranging something there may be a good many options. Some are very informal. A chat in the corridor, around the office refreshment area, half-way up the stairs or in the elevator can constitute a meeting – and be perfectly appropriate on occasions; anything else would waste time.

On other occasions some formality is appropriate. Your office is important. Can it seat the number of people you are regularly involved with (and are there adequate meeting rooms for larger gatherings – time can be wasted just looking for somewhere to meet). Many have their office furnished with a table as well as a desk, and some favour a comfortable seating area around a low table (this is nice, but may be unsuitable for some gatherings as handling paper is more difficult). Are the chairs comfortable, is there sufficient space and – in some areas still a contentious issue – can those who wish to smoke do so? These kinds of question need a thought, and several things reflect directly on how long things take, for example:

- *comfort:* too much and everyone falls asleep, but too little and the discomfort will prove disruptive. Things to consider here include not just chairs, but the amount of space available for people and papers, lighting levels, appropriate heating/ventilating, layout and shape (a long narrow room may make people at the back feel left out or render them inaudible, but most meetings of the size discussed here are probably best 'boardroom' style or, like King Arthur's knights, at a round table), ease of serving refreshments etc.

- *distractions:* remove them. No telephone calls or interruptions (except what is sanctioned, some things really do constitute an emergency). No noise, no enthralling view out across some riveting landscape. Remember every time someone is distracted and interrupts with 'sorry, can you repeat that' the meeting takes just a few moments more.

- *in or out of the office?* there are some meetings that warrant the cost, and time, of leaving the office and its distractions behind. As an example consider a senior planning meeting. It has been said already that there is often never sufficient time for planning, especially long range thinking. But it is vital – somehow it has to be fitted in or the organisation's long term development can suffer. Perhaps two uninterrupted days would make all the difference, in which case a residential session out of town over a weekend may well be justified. Something that might with the best will in the world proceed in fits and starts over some weeks or months, can be concluded satisfactorily in two days. It does not even have to be a weekend to justify this kind of approach, and there may be a variety of reasons that make it desirable, such as the need to hold a meeting on neutral ground. If the venue is chosen carefully you can have a good businesslike atmosphere and some recreational facilities as well if the time taken also provides motivational advantage. This needs thinking about. I am not suggesting you jump on an aeroplane heading for your favourite exotic destination every time you call a major meeting, but such an approach not only does have its place, but can be time efficient also.

Give your meetings the right environment and they will go more smoothly; and a meeting going smoothly will take less time than one that does not.

Lay on the right equipment and facilities

It is said that a bad workman blames his tools, but notwithstanding, if the equipment is right then the job may go better. A meeting, you may well say, is just a group of people talking. What equipment can be needed? In fact, several things may be useful, including:

- *the basics:* how many meetings have been delayed because someone asks 'Anyone have a pencil?' – too many, so it may help to supply pens/pencils, paper; also a jug of water and glasses and sometimes, as mentioned earlier, namecards and ashtrays. Pre-organised tea/coffee breaks (or heated containers or vacuum flasks in the room) will smooth the natural breaks.

- *visual aids:* even small routine meetings may use some visual aids these days. The saying that a picture is worth a thousand words is true; they are useful not only to vary the pace of the meeting, but they directly save time, one clear graph for example negating the need for a long, difficult explanation. If visual aids are used then the room will need sufficient power points so that an overhead projector (OHP), a 35mm slide projector (for these two a screen is necessary), or even a video can be used. Do make sure anything like this is tested beforehand, it is another time waster to find at the start of the meeting that a delay is necessary to change a defective bulb, or even that a marker pen that will not write must be replaced. Flipcharts or white boards are also useful and need no power source.

- *external equipment:* by this I mean what needs to be conveniently nearby. A good example is a photocopier. A common occurrence is for someone at a meeting to decide it would be useful to copy something to all present and a delay then ensues as he disappears or summons assistance, more so if the nearest machine is three floors down the building.

- *equipment for large meetings:* large numbers pose different problems and additional equipment may be needed, for example, a lectern, microphone, different (or larger) visual aids. Again all this needs preparing in advance or it can waste the time of the whole group on the day.

A well prepared and set up meeting is likely to have fewer hitches and take less time to conclude, so thought about these kinds of thing is always useful. A regular meeting room can be permanently set up with what is necessary, and standing arrangements mean that only one instruction is necessary and everything is then arranged.

Never end with AOB

This is a useful and well proven time saver (and something that will help almost any meeting go better). Any Other Business, or AOB, is that miscellany of bits and pieces, often the awkward topics, gripes, administrative details and such like, that add tedium and time to a meeting. Consider what happens. If this is taken at the end of the meeting, as the items forming this are tabled – and others are thought of – a long, rambling session can develop that extends the time well past the intended close. It also lets the meeting tail away rather than allowing the person leading the meeting to bring it to a firm and, if appropriate, punchy conclusion.

This item should be dealt with promptly. First, the Chair should remind those present what is listed under any other business. This should *not* include individual items that can be dealt with separately in discussion with two or three people, so do not need the whole group present. Any items of this sort should be firmly deferred. Then an amount of time should be allocated: 'Let's take 15 minutes to get these bits cleared up'. With the rest, and the main part, of the meeting still pending it is much easier to insist that the time is adhered to and that discussion does not become protracted over minor matters which is a sure way to risk failing to meet the meeting's main objective, or at least to take longer than necessary to do so.

Summary

Everything that has been mentioned in this chapter makes a clear point: you cannot have weak people skills and be a good time manager. The two things are simply not compatible. What is more, poor management will end up adversely affecting the time utilisation of those who work for you – and with you – as well as your own. Here we have focused on key issues involved in dealing with people in various ways, those that directly link to time and its successful utilisation. Further reading, or study, relating to the detail of management and people skills may be useful. It may be worth considering your job separately in more detail to see in which aspects of it some review might be useful in this respect. Even for experienced managers, a review of their management practices can help improve not just the results they achieve, but their productivity also.

8

On the move
Time management away from the office

'The only way to be sure of catching a train is to miss the one before it'
G. K. CHESTERTON

Travel broadens the mind, they say. It is good, it is fun and the further away and more exotic the destination the better. Offices are always full of people who, if you say you are going to Hong Kong or Toronto for the week, always say brightly: 'Have a nice time', thus demonstrating that their experience of the rigours of business travel is nil. And most of the time it is not exotic locations and first class hotels, it is Coventry and an undistinguished concrete motel. Nevertheless, the terminology sticks. A person 'on the move'; is busy, a go-getter and on the way up.

Yet the reality is that travel of all sorts is often very time consuming, and is not, in fact, always necessary. How long before the scientists have us sitting in meetings not knowing which participants are really there and which are merely projected holograms? Meantime your time effectiveness while travelling needs thinking about. Everyone's travel is different, some spending a lot of time simply going a few miles to another office of the organisation (office and factory, perhaps), others regularly spanning continents and time zones. Time can be saved by the way things are organised and time can be gained by using it effectively during the travel; here we cover some points relative to both intentions.

We start with the most fundamental question posed by this topic.

To travel or not?

Many years ago in wartime Britain posters were used to persuade the population to help the war effort in various ways. One said simply: IS

YOUR JOURNEY REALLY NECESSARY? (fuel was in short supply). This would be no bad maxim to have posted in every modern office, because thousands of journeys must be undertaken every day that are not really necessary. All over the world taxis, cars, trains and aeroplanes are taking people to places and to see people that are not strictly necessary. The attendant cost and time cannot even be guessed at.

Let us be entirely honest, if a business opportunity presents itself to travel to New York, Hong Kong, London or attend a conference at a well-known resort area, then provided you are not too cynical from too much travel in the past (overseas and long distance travel can be very hard work), then it is tempting, especially if the trip is all expenses paid and the air ticket is first class. So the first rule in this area is not to accept purely on the basis of your personal pleasure (well, perhaps you can have the occasional treat! but remember the time it takes).

Secondly, where some form of contact is necessary, consider the alternatives, for example:

- *have them come to you:* this may be possible, you may only have to suggest it or it may even be worth footing the bill, providing an overnight hotel stay; this will cost no more than you travelling in the reverse direction, and saves you time

- *send someone else:* yes, even to that attractively located conference, delegation must always be considered and is commented on elsewhere

- *telephone:* some things really can be dealt with pretty simply and you do not need to be face to face, or an initial telephone contact gets something under way and a visit can come later when the project is less tentative and time spent on it more worthwhile

- *write or, these days, fax:* the same applies here as for the telephone, though the two forms of communication are different, one producing a record; remember both may not generate such immediate or accurate understanding as a meeting

- *use technology:* for those able to afford it, modern telecommunications offer increasingly sophisticated possibilities, including telephone and video conferencing where you can be linked electronically to a group of people all able to converse and even see each other.

You do not have to be much of a mathematician to work out how much time could be saved over a year if you cut out even a small proportion of your journeys, one a month, one a week – the hours saved quickly mount up. So before you call to your secretary to get in touch with the travel agent, think for a moment. Of course some things can genuinely only be dealt with face to face and some journeys are essential – but not all.

That said, when the journey *is* genuinely necessary, there are other considerations for those with an eye on maximising the effectiveness of their time, not least timing.

Plan when to go

If you must make a visit, at least think carefully about when you go. Circumstances may dictate: the conference you plan to attend is on fixed dates and you either go then or not at all. Or something has to be seen to before a deadline (setting sensible ones and working ahead has been referred to previously). Otherwise you may have a choice. This takes us back to planning. What is the priority of the task? How does it fit in with other things? Here you have to juggle both ends a little. What are you going to be away from or miss? If your secretary or some key member of staff is away then it may be better delayed until they return (was *their* trip really necessary?).

Certain timing has very distinct time benefits, for example, travelling on a Sunday evening and staying overnight to be fresh and ready for business first thing on the Monday in another city. You may want to balance repeated inroads such as this with home and family who will rightly feel they are being placed second if it occurs too frequently. The timing can also reflect your personal style and bodyclock, if you are good in the morning for instance, you may want to get up early and travel to a 9.00 am appointment even if that takes some time. You can then get back and still have a reasonable portion of the day in your own office.

It is worth recording here that time affects cost, at least with particular forms of travel. It is a matter of deep mystery to me, for example, why airlines make ticketing regulations so complicated. But it is a fact that the same flight, from A to B, can cost widely different amounts depending on the day you travel, the time of the year, how long you stay and whether that includes a weekend. Hotels too offer different rates seasonally and at weekends, and other local conditions will apply to trains and all other forms of transport. So check, or get your secretary to do so, and then you may need to balance the two things deciding whether to pay more or go at a different time.

Timing is everything in so much and here it can present complex issues, demand compromise and is worth a moment's thought to decide what truly suits best.

Plan your journey

There are a number of considerations here and it is easy to waste time by overlooking even the basic things; I recently spent a frustrating time trying to find someone's office, ending up late for a meeting and knowing all the time that it would have taken less than two minutes to look up a city map before I left the office. Planning is a sensible, and time saving, precaution and you can usefully consider a number of things in advance:

- *location:* for simple and complex journeys alike you need to know where you are going. This helps everything from selecting the best mode of transport to which hotel to stay in once you arrive. It is useful to ask people you are to visit certain questions: for example, in most cities parking is a problem, so before you decide to drive, ask if they have a car park. If the answer is no, taxi or bus may be better, but a yes may make driving the best option.

- *method of transport:* depending on the nature of the journey there may be a considerable choice: car, taxi, bus or train; or you may have to fly for longer distances. More complex journeys present additional decisions – what is the best way into town from the airport, for example. The most comfortable is not always the quickest, of course, and you may be better sacrificing your comfort to take the bus.

- *route:* this needs deciding also. The greatest time saver here is to combine tasks that involve the same journey or are *en route*. If I am travelling from London to Singapore, I cannot do this every day and have to think about putting together a group of activities to make the time taken worthwhile, and may also think about whether it would be time effective to stop *en route* – in Kuala Lumpur or Bangkok perhaps – or go onwards to Hong Kong as part of the same trip, as two separate trips will always be more time consuming. It is just as worthwhile thinking and organising like this if you are going to the other side of town rather than a long distance.

- *class:* here again you must balance comfort and cost, but greater comfort can allow more to be done *en route* or for you to get down to work faster on arrival. For many the very considerable extra cost of even business class over economy on the airlines means careful thought is needed. You will be even fresher if on a long journey you have an extra day in a reasonable hotel before you go to work. This costs a fraction of the difference on the air ticket between classes but takes up more time.

- *packing:* this may seem an odd one, but travelling light can certainly save time (particularly if you have no check-in baggage when you fly) and you can get around more easily and quickly if you are not burdened with heavy luggage. You must also make sure you have everything with you that you may need. You cannot just call to your secretary to pass you a calculator or find a file. If these things are not there you either have to buy a new one, or have something sent, expensively, to catch up with you. Developing some good habits, maybe some checklists, can be useful.

The better you set up, and time, a journey the less it will disrupt other things in your life and your office. If you travel regularly the airlines and other travel providers offer some time saving perks to their frequent users, these include fast check in, transport to the airport, later check in times etc. Such things are worth keeping an eye open for as everything that reduces the time on a journey even a little may be worthwhile – and removes some of the hassle.

Once everything is arranged, there is the next question of how the time that is not committed had best be used.

Using travel time constructively

The next area to review if travel you must is how you can put the time spent to some use. This is another potentially very valuable area of time utilisation, and while you want and need no doubt to get some rest on journeys too, there are sometimes many, many hours over a period when, if the time you spend travelling or some of it can be put to good use, then your time management will produce greater productivity. Some take this to considerable extremes. On a recent visit to Bangkok, where the traffic is, to say the least, intense, I was told of one local senior executive who, calculating how many hours he spent each week getting from place to place around town, had replaced his company car with a van. He had a driver and, with the van furnished in the back with a desk, chair and all the necessary equipment – telephone, fax, computer and so on – was able to obtain several more valuable working hours each week while on the move; or rather while *not* on the move – the main characteristic of Bangkok traffic is how much time it spends stationary.

You do not need to take things this far, though it seems to me an eminently sensible idea, but there are several areas you might well consider.

WHAT YOU CAN DO

- *reading:* it is useful to catch up with all sorts of material, and easy to do as you go along; even a short journey may get a report or other document out of the way.
- *writing:* this needs the better conditions, but a good deal can be done (and dictating too, if you do not mind those around you hearing if you are on a plane, say – better for the car or taxi where there is some privacy).
- *computer work:* which includes word processing (my own favourite travel occupation). The advent of really portable computers, more user friendly systems and longer battery life – mine will go some 50 hours – makes this a real possibility, and you quickly get into the habit of doing this kind of work on the move and mentally pushing the surroundings into the background. (Note: there is news as I write of airlines banning laptop computers – to make you buy more drinks and headsets? This would be a disaster for me and, I suspect, many others. May I encourage any readers of like mind to say so to every airline they fly with – maybe we can prevent it before it becomes the norm.)
- *discussion:* this is clearly only for when you travel with colleagues. If you do there is no reason why you cannot schedule a proper meeting complete with agenda. Having said that I have twice in recent years got into discussion with strangers on aeroplanes with whom

I have ended up working, so maybe it is not only for working with colleagues.

- *telephoning:* mobile equipment makes this possible in many circumstances these days (though you should consider the peace and quiet of others). Indeed you can even carry modems and faxes, so the communications possibilities are considerable.
- *thinking:* this is particularly useful, you may need no papers, no equipment, only the intention and the plan to do so. I keep in my diary a list of 'thinking things', longer term issues, specifically needing no papers, so that I can turn this up when suitable moments occur.

WHERE TO DO THINGS

All forms of transport lend themselves to some of these kinds of task. You will get most done on longer journeys, and flying and train journeys provide a better, steadier work surface than a bumpy car ride. The trick is to plan to take suitable work and materials and, if you note how much you get done, you will give yourself an incentive to do this; it is really very useful. So too is work done in hotels. Again this must be fitted in reasonably with other activities, but hours can be gained here. Incidentally, do not be afraid to demand of the hotel anything that will help, for example, hotels seem to be equipping their hotel bedrooms with lower and lower wattage light bulbs. If there is not an area where you can see and work comfortably, ask for brighter bulbs or an extra lamp. Even waiting time can be put to use – there are some jobs where people seem to spend many hours sitting in other organisations' reception areas.

This is another area of good habits. If you get into the way of working like this, taking the right materials and references with you, then you will find it becomes a natural part of the way you work – and the time saving can be very considerable.

Keep in touch

When you are away from base, whatever the specific purpose and however long or short your trip, however near or far, you need a system to keep you in touch. If the wrong things are sent to you it wastes time;

if the wrong things are held back or, worse, handled incorrectly in your absence then more time will be wasted. Such a system starts therefore with the briefing of other people in your office, especially your secretary. If you do not say what the priorities are, how things should be handled then things have no hope of running smoothly. Modern communication makes things easier and longer distance absences create fewer problems as a result.

Keeping in touch is a two-way process. You need to contact your office regularly, and the information you give must be precise if instructions are to be followed accurately. Remember they will only know at that end what you tell them and long distance misunderstandings may take longer to sort out.

And do not forget the basics:

- leave a note of all your contact addresses (and fax numbers etc.)
- advise when you can be contacted and when not
- advise any changes to your arrangements as you go along
- give an idea in advance of the work load you will bring back for others and the urgency of such tasks

This is less an area of time saving than of making sure that time is not wasted because of lack of contact and information.

Consider how you can affect time utilisation in the office

Ask any secretary, and others too, and they will all say there are some jobs you can only get down to when the boss is away from the office. For example, on a trip I took during the writing of this book, my office was given a major clean up, something that would have been physically very difficult if I had been working in it – not only would I have been in the way, I would have been a nuisance, not wanting things touched. You can probably think of examples in your own office.

It is also a time to try to implement acts of delegation that you have perhaps been putting off. Let those who have remained in the office know that they are in charge (and let them know when you get back that they have done a good job, if they have, of course).

If you organise it right, things will not slow down while you are out of the office, they will speed up. Longer absences need more organising, of course, and so too does the time immediately after you get back. Your plan needs to accommodate time to review the mail, messages and other items that have come in while you were away. It can help to have a simple system for sorting this (perhaps 'urgent', 'soon' and 'if necessary' – the names matter less than the grouping of things). And you will need time to catch up with other people.

The attitude you take to this should be similar for a day out of the office as for three weeks on holiday or working overseas. Think beforehand about what the effect of the absence will be and organise things to minimise any disruption and specifically to keep productivity up; and give others the authority to keep things moving efficiently in your absence. It will all save you time in the end.

For those who undertake business at long distance, as I do, a word about the main bug bear of such trips, especially short duration ones, may be a worthwhile digression.

Beating jet lag

The first thing to say is that you cannot beat jet lag (though medical science says they are working on it); but you can minimise it to some degree. Though, as has been said, not everyone travels distances that involve this effect, the nature of business, which is more and more international these days, means that it is significant for many; certainly I rarely seem to fly on anything other than a fully loaded aeroplane. If you do long haul journeys you will know the effects they have on the system.

For all the glamour projected in travel advertisements, long haul flying, particularly in economy, is no picnic. It is tiring, cramped, uncomfortable and dehydrating. They are apt to serve you two dinners in quick succession when it is lunchtime and wake you up when you are wanting to sleep. Getting out of economy, if you can afford it, will make you somewhat more comfortable, but it will not lessen the effect of jet lag.

If you get off the aeroplane feeling like death, and there are other distinct effects such as an inability to concentrate as well as normal, then it is not advisable to go straight into the most important meeting of the trip. So what is the answer? Can you cure it? The short answer is 'no'; the only remedy is time. But there are things you can do to minimise the effect, starting with picking a flight that arrives at a time that suits you.

This really is a very individual area and everyone has their own way of dealing with the experience, from just giving up on it and drinking too much (why is it one of these that always seems to sit next to me?) to dubious potions and concoctions of vitamins. Some of the time on the flight you may well be able to use constructively, as just reviewed, and on arrival you may want to schedule a few simple tasks that do not demand any real concentration. Beyond that you need to experiment and see what suits your constitution and seems to help you.

I do not travel anything like as much as many, doing three, four or five long haul return trips each year, but it is enough to have made me think about it. I can only record here what I do in case this fits for anyone else:

- I never drink alcohol (this is every doctor's advice)
- I drink more than I think I need to (to combat dehydration)
- I never eat more than the smallest snack (this will not suit everyone, indeed airline staff are universally disbelieving of anyone refusing the meal and usually check several times); I was once told that jet lag was primarily digestive and find arriving hungry and eating the right meal going by local time definitely helps
- I sleep at the time of where I am going (I help this by going to bed a little early – or late – the night before I fly and taking a sleeping pill during the journey)

Anyway this helps *me*. You will do well to think about how you react and what helps, otherwise this is a sure time waster, and worse, you can find it affecting your performance as concentration is impaired. Experiment and see if you can make a difference here.

Now, a final thought which I hope you will never find useful.

Organising for emergencies

This is an area where we all hope nothing will need doing, but if there is any sort of emergency – an accident, illness or crime – then there is every reason to be prepared in advance. And one of those reasons is to avoid the substantial amount of time that may be wasted in sorting things out otherwise.

The first piece of advice is simple enough. Never travel abroad unless you are insured. Now many will reply to this 'No problem, the organisation sort it', but do you know how? If something occurs, do you have to fax the office even to be reminded of the name of the insurance company, or can you immediately make contact with someone local who will help? It is worth checking.

The second is a simple and wise precaution. Imagine one of the worst scenarios: you lose your wallet. What do you have to do? It is quite a list:

- advise your credit card companies (it is often more than one)
- sort out a new passports
- get more travellers' cheques
- confirm flights for which you now have no tickets
- get enough money fast enough not to have to walk to your next meeting and beg for a free lunch from your appointment

and there could be more, it may have contained telephone numbers or addresses for instance that need replacing.*

Much of the arranging you cannot avoid, but if you leave a record in your office of all the key things – credit card numbers, travellers' cheques, air tickets etc. – then one fax saying as little as 'wallet lost' will get your secretary working on your behalf and you can go off to your next meeting without pausing to worry about some of the items at all.

Let us hope that you never need any of this kind of thing, but if you do – be prepared.

---

* You may well say that some of these items should be locked in the hotel safety deposit box. Quite right, but you might lose it on the way from the airport to town.

Afterword

■

'Next week there can't be any crisis. My schedule is already full.'
HENRY KISSINGER

Making time management work is important to everyone. At worst, the alternative is a life of permanent muddle, pressure and frustration — not to mention the fact of actually achieving less than you would want or believe possible. So there are considerable advantages to getting to grips with the process, and it may be appropriate at this stage to recap the overall advantages to be gained. Principally, effective management of your time will allow you to:

- achieve greater productivity, efficiency and effectiveness
- give more focus to your efforts and bring any particular way of working that may be necessary, for example creativity, more certainly to bear
- be more likely to achieve your various objectives
- be more likely to be able to develop the job long term
- get more satisfaction and enjoyment from what you do
- find that home and family and job responsibilities fit better together

These overall statements incorporate many details from fewer missed deadlines to more time for key projects and better relationships with the people working with, or for, you in the organisation. Further, because time management affects results and efficiency so directly, it can have a direct bearing on your career progress; good time managers tend to be more successful than their less well organised peers

So, there certainly seem to be more than sufficient reasons to make it work for you. Some of the ideas that help seem very obvious and when you take them up they quickly fit in, become habits and work well without great effort. Other aspects of the process are inevitably harder. For example, shifting bad habits that a review of time management may highlight is a case in point (as anyone who has tried to, say, give up smoking will vouch). Like so much that is desirable in organisational life, being a good time manager does not just happen. It was said early on in this book that time management equates with self management, and the subsequent content has no doubt borne this out, though there may be just a few more points to be made that will assist.

For almost everyone at a particular time, improvements can be made and some of the ideas reviewed here may form a part of your own efforts to change or revise your own working practice. If it does not just happen, then it needs working at, and part of this initially for some may mean a little more investigation. This implies a little more time 'up front', but it is time that can certainly be worthwhile.

What else will help?

Time management is a perennial issue. But it is also an ideas area. No one truly reaches the point where they are so efficient that there will never again be an idea that can help them. In a sense the good time manager is not someone who has completed a process, but someone who sees their time management as an unending journey of exploration, who is *always* on the look out for new ways (or variations on old) which they can first identify, then make work for them, thus improving effectiveness just a smidgen more. Some of what makes this possible is no more than keeping your eyes open, and I do not wish to unreasonably suggest that you make formal investigation your life's work. However, especially if you are at a stage in your career where you need to adopt a more formal initiative to the process, you might usefully consider:

- *reading more about it:* you do not need to adopt the physical systems recommended (and sold) in some books unless you want, they may still have ideas you can use without that. There are articles published regularly in management journals too for which it may be worth keeping an eye open.
- *attending a – short – course:* (or have one run for your company or department), again this can act as a catalyst and help relate some of the principles to the specific issues that have to be tackled in your own organisation. It takes a day or two, but in the long term is an opportunity to make progress towards greater efficiency.
- *simply watch others:* there is no monopoly on good ideas and you may spot things others do as useful for you. Especially if you have colleagues or friends who appear to have a particularly good approach or system, ask them about the way they work – they

should have time to spend a moment telling you about it! This may be one of the best continuing ways of collecting further ideas and fine tuning what you do.

In the short term reading this book – at this point I am assuming you have read it and are not flicking through from the back – may act as a catalyst. If so there may be things you want to do now, at once, or certainly to put on your list. If so, do so, do not let the moment pass. In the longer term, if it helps foster a habit of inquiry about sources of increased efficiency that too may well be useful.

Even so, getting the most from the time you have available remains a constant battle. You will often be able to think of new ways to save time, and when you do you may kick yourself for not thinking of them before. You may be right, more likely because your job is dynamic and changes there will be new opportunities to save time as the job develops and your working pattern changes with it. This is true of all major changes, depending on where you are in your career. For example, the first time you have a secretary, when you become a manager of other people, have access to a computer, or start to travel on business – all these will change your work pattern and give you new ways to think about your time. So will small things and topical things, so you need to get into the habit of assessing changes for their potential effect on your time and its utilisation.

Such changes will not always be positive. A change in staffing may immediately put other people, including you, under pressure and make things more difficult. Collecting and testing ideas should be a conscious process. Keep a list. Try having a short brainstorming session at departmental meetings, exchange ideas and search for new ones. Hold a competition. Make it an active issue and prompt people to think about their time on a continuing basis. Think of this process as never stopping and you can go on improving your time utilisation throughout your career.

But do not necessarily adopt ideas slavishly. To ape the words of an infuriatingly popular song:

Do it your way

A strong point is worth making here and making firmly. Time management is a process, one which, as has been said a number of times, demands discipline. It does not just happen and it demands a conscious approach. On the other hand it does not consist of an unbendable set of rules; there is not only one thing to do for every particular situation. At this stage of reading I hope you will have found a number of things: first, some ideas you can use, immediately and directly, secondly, some you will have rejected as clearly not for you, and thirdly, areas that require further thinking. With these latter you conclude perhaps that there is something you can do differently, but you need to work on the precise way in which you will go about it.

This is fine. Time management may be something that you have to fight with yourself to implement and which constitutes a battle you will never win one hundred per cent, but it should not consist of individual acts you find just do not fit in with the way you work. Unless the process is run compatibly alongside the job you do then you will be in danger of finding that the process itself takes over, and that you are constantly thinking too much about what you should be doing rather than actually doing it. It is a means to meeting your ends and must fit with the way you work. There is an important caveat here. Do not allow the discomfort of some aspects of time management to become an excuse for not having a real way of tackling things. It is all too easy to end up feeling that to muddle through is in fact quicker in the long run (though it most often is not) and resisting or avoiding any system or approaches that will streamline the way you work.

Realistically there is a balance to be struck here. You do not want to set yourself such a convoluted way of working that, however efficient it might be, it is so uncomfortable that you never use it properly. But nor do you want to leave out thinking, ideas, systems and processes that will help you be more effective just because they take a little getting used to before they sit comfortably with the way you work. As long as you recognise that the overriding tendency amongst many people is to allow their existing habits to prevail, and see the danger in that, then you can actively work out a set of approaches and create new habits if necessary that suit you. Do not worry that some things recommended here and elsewhere do not fit for you (as long as you are *sure* they do not), create your own way forward, do it your way, and stick with that. This, and the habit of seeing the search for new ideas as never ending, will let you maximise time utilisation in your job.

But it will never be entirely plain sailing and there will always be some pressure, though again adopting the right attitude to this can, as with other factors, make a practical difference.

Releasing the pressure

Most jobs that are worth doing and provide any sort of satisfaction and reward are demanding (if you know an exception please let me know!). There will be busy times and there will be busier times; some pressure is to be expected. You must be organised if you are to cope with that, and ensure that you can concentrate on the key issues and produce the results your job demands. This is a prerequisite and must, as we have seen, be approached consciously and worked at.

If you have done that, if you have made sensible decisions and set clear and correct priorities then, in the short term at least, there may be no more you can do. You will not always have as long as you would wish for tasks, you do not always need to achieve perfection, and – above all – you can only really do one thing at a time. So, if you are sure you have taken all the action possible at a given moment to make things go well, relax and have confidence in the outcome. If you worry, and this is a destructive process, this just takes up more time. This is especially true of things that are now past. You cannot turn the clock back and it does little good to constantly review 'if only . . .' scenarios in your mind; experience can help you change the future but it will not change the past. There is a difference between being concerned about something, which implies active and purposeful working at it, and pure worry – which achieves nothing but ulcers.

This sort of attitude, which I believe is only practical, will help you cope with the pressures and, if you are not thrown by them, you will cope with them much better than if you are in a constant state of worry. At the end of the day, you have to live with yourself and the job you do, time management can not only help you be more effective, it can help you be more content in what you do and get more from it.

There is an important, but simply stated point to be made here about health, something that pressure of work can all too easily lead to be neglected. Long term health is one thing (and beyond our scope here – except to say that reducing pressure, as above, should avoid on-going stress in the negative sense), but more day to day health has some essentially practical implications. Deadlines and the projects that have them are important. But no one is indispensable. If you were not there then other arrangements would have to be made, other, perhaps lesser, priorities might suffer but things would for the most part work out. Yet if illness threatens (and I mean minor illnesses rather than being rushed into hospital) there is a great temptation to struggle on and this is more pronounced when an important deadline is looming.

Now I am not suggesting that you take to your bed at the first sign of every tiny sniffle, but this is worth thinking about logically. If a couple of days struggling on ends with you being away from the office for a week once you have to give in to whatever 'bug' you may have picked up, and a day off right at the beginning would have caught the thing in the bud, then this is not the most time effective way of dealing with it. Of course, it may be difficult to predict the course of minor ailments, but it is worth a moment's thought, and certainly it is often the case that the instant 'I am invaluable and must struggle on' response is not always best. Quite apart from anything else, you do not want to sneeze all over everyone for several days, then take to your bed, and, on your return, find the whole department has caught it from you and that *no one* is there.

Conclusion

At the end of the day is time management really something to bother about or is it just another management panacea, to make the gurus rich and take up time that could be better spent simply getting on and doing the job? I believe firmly that it is not just worthwhile, but essential. I hope this book has demonstrated that the time it takes to become better organised need not be prohibitive, indeed that as the habits develop, the techniques, tricks and, most important, the attitudes adopted clearly pay dividends.

It was said early on that time management means self management, and certainly most of the content of this book will have reinforced the point. What makes it all work is not simply having an understanding of the principles and enough ideas, but the discipline and ultimately the habit to make it stick as an overall way of working.

The results stemming from it have been stated. Even so, is the net effect worthwhile? I believe the answer is certainly yes. You probably spend a major part of your life on your work (proportionately more if you are *not* too well organised) so it will be important to you. It is one business technique that not only affects the organisation through the individual's job and the results it generates, but also affects the individual – *your* job satisfaction, state of mind and general well-being are all subject to the way you run things in this respect. Becoming a better time manager may take a commitment, and some working at but, as the saying has it 'there is no such thing as a free lunch' – most things that are worthwhile do need some investment of time and effort. This is no exception except perhaps in the possible return; for it is no exaggeration to say that good time management *can* change your life promptly, for the better in a variety of different ways and, if you foster the habits involved, for ever (or, more realistically, for the remainder of your career).

> *'Eternity is a terrible thought. I mean,*
> *where is it going to end.'*
>
> TOM STOPPARD

Appendix
Time management forms

∎

FORMATS TO SAVE TIME: EXAMPLES

In the course of this book I have put over something of both the philosophy of time management – the attitudes, indeed the convictions that it demands – and the how-to elements – what you can do practically to assist maximisation of the useful time you have available. Both aspects are important to making it work. And the process of undertaking a constructive approach in this area is, as has been said, continuous.

One specific and practical element that provides a basis for reminder, organisation and action is any system of formats that you may use. I have already cast some scepticism on many proprietary systems because they can be restrictive and often do not suit individuals as well as they would wish. This is a serious problem, not just of mismatch, but because it can lead to feelings ranging from inadequacy to out and out muddle as a variety of forms and procedures are shoehorned into the practicalities of a particular way of working. Such feelings can all too easily result in despair and less time and effort being spent on time management than would otherwise be the case. I have heard time management systems companies described as akin to the manufacturers of mustard (whose profit is made not from what their customers eat, but what they leave uneaten on the sides of their plates), and many expensive systems remain stillborn.

Although the system *you* need may be simple, and something you can originate from scratch, there are likely to be some key forms most managers can benefit from in one way or another. As I have said, I favour – and use – a loose-leaf system and am grateful to Filofax (whose products make up my system) for permission to reproduce some of their forms here by way of example. These are largely self-explanatory though there are comments added as necessary to make a point.

Whatever you settle on using (and it may take some experiment), the overriding requirement is that it suits *you*. Unless this is the case you will not utilise it as well, its use is less likely to become a habit – something that is so helpful with much that is necessary in time management – and you will be pushed back towards the mess of reality into which you are striving to bring order.

If your intentions are well founded, and it is the process of forming practical intentions above all that a book such as this can help clarify, then action can, and is more likely to, follow. It is *your* time. Manage it effectively and it is *you* who reap the benefit. So it is, inevitably, you who must take the initiative. Perfection may continue to elude you, but real rewards are there for the taking.

EXAMPLE 1: DIARY

This is something surely everyone must have. But there are choices to be made: day per page or week to view for instance. The example shows one page of a week to view design, usefully allowing space to note tasks separately from the timed area of the page. The system of symbols saves space and allows everyone to use the spaces for whatever *they* decide the symbol should represent.

January Janvier Januar Enero Gennaio 1994　　　　　　　　　　　　　Week 1

Monday 3	**Tuesday** 4	**Wednesday** 5
Lundi	Mardi	Mercredi
Montag (UK)	Dienstag (SC)	Mittwoch
Lunes	Martes	Miércoles
Lunedì	Martedì	Mercoledì
3–362	4–361	5–360
8	8	8
9	9	9
10	10	10
11	11	11
12	12	12
13	13	13
14	14	14
15	15	15
16	16	16
17	17	17
18	18	18
19	19	19
20	20	20
☎	☎	☎
✍	✍	✍

EXAMPLE 2: YEAR PLANNER

This can be especially useful and many people use a combination of diary pages and a pull out planner. The planner allows you to visualise the relationship of one thing with another – you can *see* how say a week overseas in March will affect and relate to events and commitments in nearby months. This gives information that is simply not forthcoming from a glance at one diary page. The example shown pulls out to about 40cm across, manageable yet with good useful space; shading on it differentiates weekdays from weekends.

	Mon	Tue	Wed	Thu	Fri	Sat	Sun	Mon	Tue	Wed	Thu
Jan						1	2	3 **1**	4	5	6	7
Feb		1	2	3	4	5	6	7 **6**	8	9	10	11
Mar		1	2	3	4	5	6	7 **10**	8	9	10	11
Apr				1	2	3	4 **14**	5	6	7	8
May						1	2 **18**	3	4	5	6
Jun			1	2	3	4	5	6 **23**	7	8	9	10
Jul				1	2	3	4 **27**	5	6	7	8
Aug	1 **31**	2	3	4	5	6	7	8 **32**	9	10	11	12
Sep			1	2	3	4	5 **36**	6	7	8	9
Oct					1	2	3 **40**	4	5	6	7
Nov		1	2	3	4	5	6	7 **45**	8	9	10	11
Dec				1	2	3	4	5 **49**	6	7	8	9

©1993 *FILOFAX*® Ref.385594

JANUARY
```
WK  M  T  W  T  F  S  S
52              1  2
 1  3  4  5  6  7  8  9
 2  10 11 12 13 14 15 16
 3  17 18 19 20 21 22 23
 4  24 25 26 27 28 29 30
 5  31
```

FEBRUARY
```
WK  M  T  W  T  F  S  S
 5     1  2  3  4  5  6
 6  7  8  9 10 11 12 13
 7  14 15 16 17 18 19 20
 8  21 22 23 24 25 26 27
 9  28
```

MARCH
```
WK  M  T  W  T  F  S  S
 9     1  2  3  4  5  6
10  7  8  9 10 11 12 13
11  14 15 16 17 18 19 20
12  21 22 23 24 25 26 27
13  28 29 30 31
```

APRIL
```
WK  M  T  W  T  F  S  S
13              1  2  3
14  4  5  6  7  8  9 10
15  11 12 13 14 15 16 17
16  18 19 20 21 22 23 24
17  25 26 27 28 29 30
```

EXAMPLE 3: DAY PLANNER

Many find this a useful form. Undated and with room for Action points as well as appointments, it can be used independently or interleaved with the diary element of a system. The example allows action to be specified (e.g. letter or telephone) with a tick and has a column to mark completion and space for other specified notes at the foot of the page.

	⌛	✉	☎	Action	✓
8					
9					
10					
11					
12					
1					
2					
3					
4					
5					
6					
7					
8					

EXAMPLE 4: ACTION SHEET

These can be a key element of many a system, providing a flexible way to prompt, prioritise and record action.

Action

EXAMPLE 5: MEETINGS PLANNER

This form prompts the formalisation of all the key aspects of a meeting (earlier in the book these were clearly identified as taking up a major part of many people's work time). Using symbols the form has space for the basic details: date, start and finish time and also: agenda, sub agenda, attendees, objectives, delegated tasks, pre and post meeting notes. Few meetings would not benefit from more preparation. Something like this can prompt the process and make it quicker to undertake.

	✓
1	
2	
3	
4	
5	
6	
7	
8	
9	
10	

EXAMPLE 6: EXPENSES SHEET

Something we all have to worry about in both business and private life is money; and it demands accurate records. This form uses symbols to facilitate the recording of the date and amounts of expense items, and also to identify whether they involve cash, credit card or cheque, and has room for additional notes.

The examples shown are but a fraction of possible forms. Others available include those designed for:

- recording names, addresses and telephone and/or fax numbers
- analysis sheets
- expenses specific to car or travel
- planning sheets for specific activities such as telephone calls
- customer records

and these and more can be integrated with a variety of other information sheets (for example, a map of the London Underground) and other devices ranging from plastic wallets for credit cards to envelopes in which to collect the receipts that must so often accompany expenses, all clipping into the same loose-leaf binder. As has been said a loose-leaf system, including a diary, is almost a prerequisite for good time management.

FLEXIBILITY

While the task is to create a set of forms that works for *you*, the permutations of what is available in printed form is considerable, and most people will probably be able to find something that suits and which needs minimal amendment. The range offered by Filofax makes the point. Their various systems come in four sizes so whether you want something that you can carry about – either in your back pocket or a jacket – or something larger to use as a desk system or carry in a brief case, there is one to suit. Many people use a combination; certainly in my own case I have a number of forms with me in a wallet-sized file I carry in my jacket pocket, and this is expanded with a desk size system. The particular forms reproduced here are unique to the latest Filofax system which is called 'Filofax System Organiser' and which is based on A5 size pages punched in with the now ubiquitous six holes. The full kit includes the option of a divided filing box as well as a wallet, the two together providing still more flexibility in how, as Filofax put it: you *plan it, do it* and *record it*.

Postscript

■

In view of the topic of this book, it is worth adding a few words about its writing. I have, in the last couple of years, had two books published by Pitman Publishing: *Marketing for Non-marketing Managers*, in this same series linked to the Institute of Management, and the more specialist *Marketing Professional Services* (published in the *Financial Times*/Pitman Publishing series).

Writing a book seems, to me at any rate, a somewhat daunting task. However, once this title was agreed, I got down to work, first reviewing my own work habits (and ignoring my secretary's insistent 'Much help that will be'), conducting some informal research and planning out the sequence and content of the book before starting to draft the text.

By coincidence, almost as soon as I began I had an assignment scheduled in Malaysia and, working on a portable word processor, found myself drafting the first few pages in the cramped seat of a jumbo jet. For interest I kept a note of where subsequent work took place over the following weeks that were involved in completing the manuscript; where other than at my desk, that is. It included a number of planes, several trains (but no cars or buses – they are too bumpy and I cannot hit the correct keys). It included some of the many hours that those journeys entailed spending in airports and railway stations (here the airport restaurant is often best, a desk-height table, often an electric plug near enough to use – ignoring the occasional odd look – and refreshment to hand). It also included various locations in several hotels – not only bedrooms, but coffee shops, business centres, lounges and, in South East Asia where I work regularly and the climate allows, by the swimming pool – the living room at home, relations' dining rooms on family visits and a restaurant where I waited interminably to meet someone who was very late.

This accounted for probably two thirds of the 70,000 or so words you have now read. Although the 'polishing' took place primarily in my office, it made the drafting a more productive process, fitting in better with other work and allowing me to complete the writing over a shorter period of time than would have otherwise been the case and thus maintain a greater continuity of thought.

This is not, incidentally, intended to make out I am a workaholic; most of the above would otherwise have been wasted time, and besides there is a satisfaction in writing. But I was going to end by saying this was an appropriate example of effective time management in action; certainly it led to my discovering the ultimate put-off to people interrupting: 'Will it wait? I am working on my time management book'.

Index

assessing current use of time, 9, 12, 17
appointments, 20, 40
anticipation, 27
abstracts, 46
agenda, 135
AOB, 143

batch filing, 94
batching tasks, 39
biological clock, 43
breaks, 45
bring forward file, 52
'black hole', jobs, 84
brevity, 89
bulletin board, 91
briefing, 114

control, 12, 127
communication, 12, 51, 89, 114, 117
creativity, 31
cherry picking, 46
checklists, 53
computers, 64, 87, 95, 112
chron-file, 94
copying, 88
conflict, 110
consultation, 128

deadlines, 78, 80
delegation, 5, 29, 115
diary, 20, 22, 40, 51
disorganisation, 37
difficult tasks, 61
dual reporting, 112

entertaining, 109

fax, 71, 88
filing, 40, 92
favourite tasks, 63

habits, 3, 6
home, 34

highlighting, 47
investment of time, 5, 29
implementation, 10
interruptions, 60, 64, 140
information storage, 97

job description, 76
jetlag, 153

lunch, 108

Murphey's laws, 7
monitoring, 12
messages, 22
miscelleny, 81
methodology, 81
memos, 90
measles test, 91
management by walking about (MBWA), 107
managing others, 112
motivation, 126
meetings, 131

'no', 31

objectives, 23, 76
organisation, 37
over engineering, 63
office politics, 111

Pareto's law, 75
'parking' documents, 52
panic, 28
paperwork, 43, 52, 87
prompt file, 52
perceptions, 2, 71, 83
performance standards, 48
planning, 10, 20, 38, 54
pending, 52
planning chart, 27
perfection, 32

productivity, 34
priorities, 39, 75, 85
project files, 44
people, 105

quality, 33, 48

results (of time management), 2
rolling plan, 20
reactive time, 21
reading, 46
reports, 99
recruitment and selection, 113

setting objectives, 23, 25
self-motivation, 35
secretaries, 50, 93
scheduling, 78
systems, 82, 127
stress, 85
synergy, 92
socialising, 106
swapping tasks, 121

things you do not like, 62

timing, 136
teamwork, 35
training, 122
time (amount saved), 4
time equation, 4
time trap, 6
time log, 16, 18, 19
timewasters, 60
time management profile, 14
time management systems, 22, 163
time management goals, 35
thinking ahead, 27
thinking time, 30
telephone interruptions, 69
telephone calls, 71, 88
travel, 145

urgency, 77
unnecessary tasks, 83

visitors, 64

work plan, 20
writing, 99, 100
wastebin, 103